ISBN 978-1-331-85722-8
PIBN 10242913

For support please visit www.forgottenbooks.com

English
Français
Deutsche
Italiano
Español
Português

www.forgottenbooks.com

Mythology Photography **Fiction**
Fishing Christianity **Art** Cooking
Essays Buddhism Freemasonry
Medicine **Biology** Music **Ancient**
Egypt Evolution Carpentry Physics
Dance Geology **Mathematics** Fitness
Shakespeare **Folklore** Yoga Marketing
Confidence Immortality Biographies
Poetry **Psychology** Witchcraft
Electronics Chemistry History **Law**
Accounting **Philosophy** Anthropology
Alchemy Drama Quantum Mechanics
Atheism Sexual Health **Ancient History**
Entrepreneurship Languages Sport
Paleontology Needlework Islam
Metaphysics Investment Archaeology
Parenting Statistics Criminology
Motivational

astery o   en
and Nations

BY

ALBION ELI SMITH

"Prove all things; hold fast that which is good."—Paul.

PRINTED FOR THE AUTHOR
BY THE METHODIST BOOK CONCERN, CINCINNATI, OHIO

It lies within the power and province of humanity to build a highway over which the childhood of the whole world can safely travel and reach a noble manhood and womanhood. The aim of this book is to point out the abundant means and material which have been provided for constructing such a highway.

We undertake to live and make ourselves content with that degree of comfort which is possible for all the world to have who will work as hard as we do, waste no more than we do, and be as easily satisfied as we are with what is reasonable and possible for the multitude to have.

This book is dedicated to the busy people the world around who are doing life's necessary work, and who have helped to make our travels possible and comfortable; with the hope and belief that it will assist in opening the doors of opportunity to all children, and will aid in placing within their reach the great essentials for a noble manhood and womanhood.

CONTENTS

CONTENTS

CONTENTS

7

CONTENTS

PREFACE

SINCE the time of history, the talent, devotion, and perseverance expended in striving for better things has been enormous; yet, in spite of all this labor, sacrifice, and suffering endured in wars and persecutions in the name of God and humanity, how vast the catalogue of wrongs and misfortunes which beset humanity to-day!

The slow progress of the forces of good against the powers of evil since the coming of Christ, nineteen hundred years ago, convinced me long since that some vital errors are lurking in the methods of carrying out the Redeemer's plans to save the world, and years ago I began a diligent search to detect those errors and discover the truth. The formulas under which I have studied the problems of life are the following questions:

What is wrong with myself?

What is wrong with my neighbor?

What is wrong with the Churches and reformers?

What is wrong with the world in general?

The two inquiries which naturally follow these questions are:

Who is to blame in each case?

What is the remedy?

After searching diligently for many years, I have found out what has been of inestimable value to me, and as the principles involved are of universal application, I assume that they can be equally valuable to others.

The first draft of this book was written while I was traveling and constantly seeing the abuses which are keeping the people in weakness and ignorance in foreign countries. My impressions were thus emphasized by the conditions about me, and this fact explains the stress laid on some practices which may be regarded as of minor importance by those unfamiliar with other parts of the world. As I have given my time and effort to studying the people in as many countries and in as many conditions of life as possible, I have not yet been at liberty to make myself well acquainted with the literature bearing directly on the subjects treated in the following pages. Being written in part as a diary, it must discuss different subjects somewhat as they occurred to me in travel, and not entirely after a topical arrangement. With the efficient help of my wife, as together we have gone over every line in review, I have labored hard to keep this volume of very moderate size, without sacrificing too much valuable material contained in the first writing. By this effort I believe we have retained only what the public will find well worth reading

The purpose of this book is to encourage and preserve the good and true wherever these are found, and it would gladly aid any persons or institutions to free themselves from the false and erroneous. It assumes that it is no privilege to a person in any position whatsoever to be allowed through the force of circumstances to continue to wrong himself and others. *Surely no one has the right to teach a child false doctrine and errors in religion or anything else.* If the practices and lives of any persons are condemned, it is solely that childhood may be protected from wrong. We want the truth, at whatever cost, whether in money, in effort, or in sacrificing the cherished traditions of the past.

The author does not boast that this book is original. He has traveled far, studied long, and labored hard to make it a faithful interpretation of the Original.

AN APPEAL TO BUSY MEN

"Divinely fashioned man, best work of God,
Made in His image, life-breath of His soul:
How canst thou love the soil beneath thy feet
More than thy fellow-man?"

"The earth is fair,
And beautiful its fields of waving grain;
Its iron strong, its gold and diamonds rare.
Its Maker called it 'good.'   Why should not I?"
"Yes, fairer than the morning is the earth;
Yet lovlier far the children of thy home,
That will be men and women ere the sun
Has numbered many journeys in his course.

"You delve among the jewels of the mine,
You follow plow or reaper day by day;
You spend long years amid the noise and din
And whir of factory wheels, to gather wealth.
Oh busy, anxious man! have you forgot
Those little ones, part of your better self,
To whom belongs your first and greatest care?
Too oft they wander from your heart and home,
And many go astray while you pursue
Some fleeting, fading bauble in the mart.

"You rush with feverish haste and anxious brow,
To field or mine or market, lest perchance,
Some other hand should grasp the envied prize.
And why such haste?   That you may soon return
Laden with treasures for the ones you love?
Alas! the tempter in your absence came
And stole the heart, and wrecked the youthful life.

"While you were busied with those lesser things,
Did you forget that little hands and feet
Need guidance, lest they go astray and break
The heart that loved them, but bestowed its first
And best attention on the things that fade?

II

APPEAL

"Oh brother man, be just!   To Cæsar give
All Cæsar's due, but render God His own.
For your best love He gave those little ones,
That in their noble lives, led by your care,
They might bring honor to His name and yours.
What God loves most is worthiest of thy love.
Be faithful to this trust and thou shalt know,
When kindred earth receives again the form
In which you served mankind and honored God,
He then will greet thy spirit with 'Well done!
Earth toils are past, life's victories are won.' "

—ALBION ELI SMITH.

INTRODUCTION

COULD I have one supreme wish granted, it would be to make conditions such that every child born into this world would be intelligent, strong, trustworthy, and free. No such wish will ever be granted me, but there is a lesser privilege that is practical. A pathway that has been traveled by one ordinary person can become a highway for the multitude. I have traveled far and wide to get acquainted with my fellow beings in foreign lands. I went to see them and live among them for a brief time, feeling that they were all my neighbors, and now this neighborly feeling is the uppermost sentiment in my mind as I meet the people of any land, either here or elsewhere.

In my travels and studies of the later years I have been seeking the shortest path to a useful, happy life that may be followed by the children of every country. What some genius here and there might do has no bearing on my problems and does not deflect the needle of my compass. Those who have plenty of money or a special gift in some direction may by these means secure special favors, but the great crowd of humanity can not follow them. My claim is not that I have done an unusual thing, and others can not equal it; but that I have done an unusual thing, and everybody can do as well or go far enough to secure great benefits. There are forces and means within reach of humanity which make it practical and feasible to give to every child a good degree of all the privileges I have enjoyed. Not that all should do the same as I have done—people will never become like quails, each one looking and acting just like the rest—but all can become strong, capable, and honest, all can become good citizens. I have used

13

my travels to illustrate a great principle, not to serve as a mold into which every person must be crowded. My experience would give every one the freedom to do what he would like to do, and then he can make whatever use he prefers of the money or other powers thus placed within his hands. He may travel, go to college, buy a farm, or simply lay aside his accumulations and decide later what use he will make of them.

I have gathered ideas and practices from different parts of the earth, and tested their value for the average person. My aim has been to know whether human nature is so much alike the world over that a composite life might be constructed by choosing the best knowledge from many peoples, incorporating this into one life and holding that one up as a general model for all mankind. I have no hesitation in stating positively that this can be done. So many millions are living the simple life, with no thought of suffering or sacrifice, that that principle is established. These are strong and vigorous, and if they are behind other people in any respect, it is not due to their simple mode of life; other causes are to blame for any defects in their fiber or character. So many persons in the varied ranks of life have denied themselves for others and worked on faithfully with little concern for their own comfort that the fact of such a possibility is thoroughly proved.

The thinking world will surely agree with me when I say there have been numerous cases of heroic fidelity scattered all along man's pathway, from the earliest times to the present; the fault is, there have been too few of them. The point of importance is, can their kind become the rule instead of the exception? Can conditions so change that the multitude will be going the right way, and only a few stragglers going the wrong way? I say most emphatically, they can. When one steamboat had crossed the ocean it proved the possibility of such a voyage. Now the waters of the Atlantic hardly become quiet from the churning of one propeller before another follows in its wake. I believe all good things should become common, especially good men and women; and one great object of this writing is to offer my experiences and my studies in proof of this statement.

The purpose of this book is in no sense to give a detailed account of my travels. Far more skillful pens have described the different countries and peoples of the world. My aim is to show the triumphs of certain principles over what have been considered great difficulties, and to prove how easy and universal these triumphs may become. Travel on the earth used to be very slow and difficult; now it has become rapid and comfortable. The journey of life on the way to satisfactory happiness and contentment has been and still is uncertain and perplexing. A few find the way; many travel only a short distance, and half give up; while still more fail utterly to reach the goal. The success of temporal things by right principles proves the possibility of the success of spiritual things by right principles.

ECONOMY OF SELF-MASTERY.

A host of good people are paying a dollar for fifty cents' worth of comfort. The reader of this book will see that the author has learned to get a dollar's worth of comfort out of fifty cents.

My wife and I have undertaken to live and make ourselves content with that degree of comfort which is possible for all the world to have who will work as hard as we do, waste no more than we do, and be as easily satisfied as we are with what is reasonable and possible for the multitude to have.

We have needed food, lodging, clothing, and traveling expenses. The emphasis must be laid not on the travel, but on the principles of economy involved, and those who stay at home could consequently have more money for some other purpose.

INTRODUCTION

I give here the figures for our several journeys, which are more fully described in Chapter XVII, to show what it is possible for one to do by following the self-mastery system.

My first journey was a tour of the world covering a distance of 30,000 miles and one year's time, at a cost of something over $800. For convenience I speak of it as $70 per month, which is above the actual cost.

My second trip was from Puebla, Mexico, southward along the coast, and somewhat into the interior of Central America; then to Panama; thence across the Isthmus and up through the West Indies, visiting Jamaica and taking the greater length of Cuba. From Havana I went northward through Florida and the Atlantic States to Washington. With side-trips, I traveled 5,000 miles in three months' time at a cost of $180, or $60 per month.

My third trip was from Munich, Germany, *via* Vienna and Warsaw to St. Petersburgh; thence returning *via* Koenigsburg, Posen, and Berlin to Munich. With side-trips, the distance covered was 2,900 miles in one month's time, at a cost of $50.

I will give the journeys of myself and wife in three sections, as this method best illustrates the principles of economy involved.

At the end of ten and a half months we reached Munich, Germany, having visited Ireland, France, Spain, Algiers, and Italy. My wife had traveled 8,670 miles, and I had traveled 9,500 miles, at a combined cost of $500.

At the end of one year I had added my Russian trip, which made the figures 8,670 miles for my wife, who remained in Munich, and 12,400 miles for myself. The whole year's expenses for two persons was $586.

Then going northward through Germany, Holland, Belgium, and England, at the end of fourteen months, when we had reached Wisconsin, my wife had traveled 15,400 miles and I 19,000 miles, at a cost of $800 for both. For convenience we call it $60 per month, which more than covers all expenses, including some clothing for each of us.

These journeys were of such an extent, and were taken under such a variety of circumstances, as to make them of real value in testing the system. We did not feel pinched: we provided our own good, wholesome food and led a free life generally. I should not like to mislead any one into thinking that this was a simple matter. It required a knowledge of the languages of the country, experience in travel, and a good degree of mastery over one's tastes and desires, or one would not be entirely satisfied as he goes along. People do remarkable things and endure hardships of all kinds on a wager. Our experiments have little in common with that, except in being controlled by a great purpose. Our great purpose had much to do with our being content and enjoying life as we lived it from day to day.

It will be of interest to note the cost to us of a list of things which to many people figure up quite a sum. In fourteen months' time our combined expenses did not exceed one dollar for the following items: Drives, dances, theaters, operas, shows, wine, beer, or any liquor, tobacco, tea, coffee, ice-cream, and soda-water. We boiled the water if it was not safe to drink without boiling, and we required no medicine. If it be urged that at our age we did not need certain of these things, I reply that this depends not on the age, but on the training. You have heard the adage, "There is no fool like an old fool." It depends on where the mastery in any person is centered, whether in his spirit and his best judgment or in his animal nature, making him a slave to a dozen different appetites and habits; and also whether he finds a great sufficiency in the companionship of his near friends, and in other people generally. I find a great deal of satisfaction in the companionship of my Maker, my better self, my wife, and also in the company of whatever fellow-beings I live among at any time or place. In all my journeyings I was not conscious of denying myself, but rather of having an unusual freedom and of choosing the best course.

For some place to go we attended public meetings and religious and other gatherings in connection with Churches and missions. Here we met many congenial people and made numerous friendships. Some would say these are rather dry places. That depends on one's power of appreciation of values. Some persons I have met spend time and money in places that are entirely too wet for one of my tastes and training; much depends on the ideal of companionship which rules. To be explicit, I went where I thought my Great Companion would go, and kept away from the places I thought He would avoid, and found it to my advantage financially and socially, and to my entire personal satisfaction in every way. This, to me, does not mean an ascetic or monkish life, but simply taking the course dictated by the best wisdom and by sound common sense.

It is now my purpose to give the principles by which so much can be accomplished with so little money. In these times of universal complaint of high prices and consequent privation and discontent, it is important to know one's possibilities and limitations, and also to realize the privileges lying within reach of the multitude. The few who have plenty of money may think this does not concern them, but in view of the present popular unrest it is well worth their time to seriously ponder these problems and help teach the disaffected people to use common sense rather than dynamite in getting their rights.

THE PRINCIPLES BY WHICH MY PRIVILEGES HAVE BEEN SECURED.

I must have the intelligence to know what to do in different circumstances and conditions.

I must wait on myself, and not be dependent on others for little things; I must be capable of doing whatever is necessary.

I must have the courage to live within my means—small means, some would call them. I must not be ashamed of the virtues of economy. I must see that it is a mark of the savage, and not of distinction, to spend money in personal extravagance, as though it had no value.

I must be content with what the millions of busy people the world over have, and find sufficient in the matter of personal comforts.

I must teach myself to be satisfied with a small amount of any luxury, such as expensive food, clothing, or conveniences. The type of the soldier's life is in my mind and has for me turned many dollars into wiser channels and given me the mastery of circumstances.

I must be in a good degree a self-master, able to police myself, to support myself, and to pension myself.

THE KEY TO THE SITUATION.

I must believe there has been a complete self-master who, with all possible paths open to him, chose the best one for him and every person to follow from the standpoint of common sense, business, health, and happiness. In other words, he did the things he did and in that particular manner because it was the right way and the best way to do them. This was the Infinite Man, Christ Jesus, who lived an actual man among men, and by His example and words taught the great principles of life. Because He, the Infinite Man, was entirely successful in His sphere, I, a finite man, can be successful in mine by the aid of His example and the help of His infinite spirit in directing my finite spirit. In doing this I must have a definite knowledge of Him, I must have His companionship, I must co-operate with Him, and I must have His help to get the mastery of my desires.

Jesus of Nazareth lived among the common people, shared their simple fare and accommodations, and engaged in the same labors in which they were employed. All this time He was in touch and close sympathy with them, yet independent of their sins and follies. He did this by the principles of self-mastery and the power of a great purpose which every human being can have. His companionship and His inspiration make me more than content to share the average personal comforts of my fellow-men, and if anything is not good enough for me, to use my strength and money to make it better for all, rather than to simply lift myself above discomfort and let the masses go to ruin. His companionship makes me comfortable in body and triumphant in mind while sharing the plain fare of my brother who speaks a different language, has a different-colored skin, and whose less cultured manners would otherwise be intolerable to me. Jesus was not satisfied with those people as they were, but He lived in the future of what all are to be when His life and teaching become the universal standard.

Self-Mastery of Men and Nations

CHAPTER I

THE ESSENTIALS OF THE SELF-MASTERY SYSTEM

SELF-MASTERY is the system of life and government which is based on absolute truth and reality, and these are made known by the co-operative action of true Religion, true Education, true Business, and true Science. This system means the complete control and development of one's self and the resources of the earth, and requires every one to do his part and to take no more than his share. The self-master must be able to police himself, to support himself, and to pension himself.

The great essentials of self-mastery are intelligence, capability, honesty, and freedom.

Intelligence means that one must have the knowledge necessary for his use and for any service he may have to perform.

Capability means that one can do whatever is required of him, that he has the usual senses and the strength and skill to employ them in actual work.

Honesty means that one can be trusted. He will not do less than his part of the work or service, and he will not take more than his share of the desirable things, whether it be money, honor, power, or anything of value that men desire to possess. One may do more than his part and take less than his share. The world is advanced by the services of this class, and it is retarded by those who do less than their part and take more than their share. An honest person who lives to maturity must by some useful

21

activity, which helps and does not harm humanity, earn and return to the world as much as he or she gets from the world's supplies and consumes in personal expenses during life; otherwise that person is sponging on the labors of others, and living as a parasite. Being born rich or poor, prince or peasant has nothing to do with one's obligation to support himself and not sponge on others.

HONESTY ILLUSTRATED.

Here are two bins of wheat: one contains sixty measures, and is to be carried by twelve men to a certain storehouse; the other contains twelve measures, and is to pay for the work. Twelve rations are ready in the dining-room. The men must do all this one at a time, and each must go in alone, measure his own load and his own pay, and take his dinner alone. Will each of these men measure out his load fairly, and divide to himself no more than his share of the pay and the food? If these are all honest, the last man will have a little less to carry, and will get his full pay and dinner, because each of the others will be careful to require himself to do his full part of the work, and take no more than his share of the pay and the food.

The great question for each human being to ask is this: "Could the world trust me to be the first to measure and divide to myself my load and my pay, and take my dinner; would they dare to be the last one with eleven others like me ahead of them?" If I am a strictly honest man or woman, the world could safely take the twelfth chance in this supposed case which covers the whole range of life's service, labor, and reward. You could trust eleven persons like Jesus of Nazareth to precede you. All ranks and conditions of people can accept this definition of honesty, and nothing less than this will satisfy the needs of human beings who must all measure up to the divine image.

The merchant is required by law and by honesty to give full weight and measure, and to pay in honest money. Then any one who does any service in the street, the factory, or in any governmental or other office is bound by the principles of honesty to give a full day's measure of service, and neither cheat in time nor shirk on his job. An honest man must give a reasonable equivalent for whatever he receives from others, or else he would have to live by gifts and be placed in the beggar class, or he must live by dishonesty and be classed as a criminal. If a man receives a fortune from his parents, uses it wisely, and then passes it on to others, he can be an honest man. If he consumes that fortune on himself, he has not given an equivalent for what he received; he can not be called an honest man.

Again, there is another side. The tradesman, the cabman, and the carman are not allowed to overcharge. There is expected to be a standard price for their services or commodities; a greater charge is dishonest. Then, plainly, the exorbitant charges of some doctors and lawyers are dishonest. Both these professions claim that they can charge rich men more than others. If so, then one of two things is implied: either that the rich man has gotten his wealth dishonestly and consequently should pay more, or that those who pay less are in the pauper class and must have a portion of their bills remitted in the name of charity. If the rich man is to pay more for doctors and lawyers, why not more for eggs, street-car fare, and everything else? In that case there would have to be an indefinite list of different prices on all commodities, gauged by the wealth of the purchaser. That would simply carry the customs of those doctors and lawyers to a full consistency, and would be to adopt the ways of the Orient, where each gets all the purchaser can be made to pay. If the members of these professions can not live without such discrimination, let them help to do away with poverty and injustice, and then all can pay for needed services.

Freedom, or liberty, means the permission to do right. It means the permission to do what every one may do without harm to any one. Freedom can not include the permission to do wrong to another in any degree, because this would open the way for a combination against the offender, and he would be thus deprived of his liberty by the use of his liberty, which is contradictory to itself. Freedom to one can never mean the bondage of others. Any wrong-doing leads finally into bondage to that wrong. Teaching others to follow the principles of freedom promotes one's own freedom; teaching others to follow the principles of bondage leads one into bondage.

Freedom belongs primarily to the realm of the spirit rather than the body. The body is the natural servant of the spirit. The body is animal, and as such must compete with other animals. Brute force is the power by which the animal rules, and two or more can vanquish one by its use. Sin and ignorance are the only enemies capable of mastering the spirit. Several spirits can not combine and conquer one, except through the agency of sin and ignorance. I am inclined to believe sin is the only final enemy that can remain master, since whosoever committeth sin is the servant of sin. Satan can not master even a child unless he first persuades him to sin. The child is, after that, in bondage to his own sin until released from it by divine power. The only way God can set a man free is to forgive or release him from past sins, and get him to stop sinning. To be kept free, knowledge is necessary, or he will again blunder into all sorts of trouble.

God is the only absolutely free being. He is made free by His complete knowledge and by His not committing any sin. Jesus, the Son of God, was absolutely free in spirit, but not in body. His body was subject to the animal law of brute force. Why could not His spirit protect His body? Because His spirit could not do what was wrong for every one else to do. That is to say, He could not kill others in self-defense, and protect Himself in that way. Christ must conquer by the principles of freedom and righteousness. His mission was not to master others, and keep order by that means, but to keep order by teaching and equipping each one to master himself. Jesus, as the Founder of the true system, could not protect His body by force and keep His spirit from sin. Had He done so, He would by that act have entered the arena on the level of any other brute force, which would mean mastery by the strongest.

Jesus said, "Ye shall know the truth, and the truth shall make you free." In this He gave to men the key to eternal life and to universal happiness. So soon as man is ready to know and practice this truth, so soon will the whole race be free. Christ is free to do what He wishes to do because He wishes to do only what is right. Our only hope is in becoming like Him in righteousness, and that will include freedom. Then we shall be "made in the image of God." Then we shall be permitted to do as we choose, because, like Jesus, we prefer to do right, and God can trust us with all freedom.

Personal Liberty. The fallacy of so-called personal liberty is this: It is the permission to do as one pleases without regard to others. One claims the privilege of getting drunk. He is then liable to commit any crime that drunkenness leads to. This same liberty must allow all his neighbors to get drunk also. Now, surely some of them will do him harm; if all keep sober, by the law of truth that makes one free, all will be free from any harm from drunkenness.

Free Belief. There are those who claim the freedom to believe or to disbelieve any statement. Plainly, no one has the right to believe a falsehood or to doubt the truth. Either of these would rob a man of his freedom and make him a slave of error. If I claim the right to believe I can go north from Boston and reach the equator, I shall soon be in bondage to my error. If I believe I can keep strong and well on a diet of mixed bran and sawdust, I shall become bound by the weakness that will follow. The same is true of any error of believing a falsehood or disbelieving the truth. When Jesus says, "The truth shall make you free," and a man doubts His word, and says he does not believe that, and proceeds to trample on the rights of others, he will soon find himself in trouble, and in bondage to his own doubts. To believe a lie or to doubt the truth are not in the direction of freedom, but of bondage. It is every man's imperative duty not only to seek to know the truth, but also to believe it. Freedom not only permits but requires every one to believe all that is true, whether it be the abstract statement of truth or whether it be the truth made real in the life of some worthy person. I am not at liberty to doubt the good or to believe in the false that is found in any person or system of doctrine. Whether I like that person or system, or whether I hate them, has nothing to do with the problem. The truth that I hate can make me free in its sphere, and the falsehood or error that I love can make me a slave in its sphere. Here again the necessity of knowledge comes in, and to know, one must not be bound by prejudice or by hatred of the truth, or he will not learn to know that truth. He must be free to learn and accept the truth, wherever it may be found.

Agencies of the Self-mastery System.

The agencies by which man is to develop and perfect the whole race can be classed under four heads: Education, Religion, Business, and Science. The order of arrangement is not important, as all must work together for the race, and every person must employ them all in his individual life. In the first place, there is imperative need of having standard definitions of these departments, stating clearly what is true and false education, true and false religion, and the same of business and science. We have standard money-values, and standard weights and measures, and by means of these the whole civilized world transacts business readily, and commerce advances. The same can be done in religion and education so soon as these two become standardized and placed on a common-sense basis, as has already been done in business matters. We are told that educated criminals are worse than ignorant ones, which is evident. It is also true that an ignorant man, though good, is incapable of doing much for the world. He makes a safe door-keeper; but there is pressing need of good men in all high places of power.

Each of these four agencies must work under the guidance and restraint of the other three. Science can discover dynamite, and education can teach an unprincipled man how to wreck his neighbor's building and destroy much property and many lives. Business can furnish plenty of men and material to put up another building. Religion comes to teach us that every man must respect the rights of his fellow-man. Laborers and capitalists might carry on war to the death of both, and desolate the earth, without the help of religion to teach them to do right and be honest with each other.

RELIGION.

Religion comes from a Latin word, *religare,* to bind or bind back, because it binds man to his Creator and his fellow-men. Religion can be defined as that department of human activity which concerns a man's relation and duty to God, his relation and duty to his fellow-men, and his relation and duty to himself. In his relation to God, man is formed after his Maker's image, and is the crowning glory of His workmanship. His duty to God is to satisfy the design and purpose of his Maker by being a faithful co-worker in developing himself and the earth, and in shaping the childhood of the world after the divine image.

Man's relation to his fellow-man is that of brother, partner, or neighbor. Man's duty to his fellow-man is to be a good brother, a good neighbor, or a good partner, as circumstances may require.

Man's relation to himself is to be master of himself. His duty to himself is to make a strong, true man of himself.

Much of the confusion and friction that exists among good men in religious matters is occasioned by a faulty definition of religion. True religion is as essential to man's spiritual nature as pure food is for his body. He can not perform the simplest act toward his fellow-men without touching the principles which bind him and his fellow-men together as related human beings. Religion is in part the continuance of common useful acts and the principles of every-day life carried to greater maturity and perfection in the higher development of the spiritual nature. The foundation principles of prayer, repentance, conversion, faith, sacrifice—in short, the whole religious vocabulary as found in the New Testament—are a part of every worthy life. Jesus was the only perfectly religious man, because He is the only one who has entirely fulfilled the requirements of His relation and duty to God, to His fellow-men, and to Himself. The person who has a false religion occupies a false relation to God, to his fellow-men, and to himself. Mohammed was false to God and he was false to his fellow-men; he slew men and degraded women. He was a slave to his own animal nature, and instead of a man, he made a beast of himself. The true followers of Mohammed imitate the life of Mohammed, and the true followers of Christ imitate the life of Christ.

EDUCATION.

The root-idea of education means to lead one out from a state of ignorance into that of knowledge. It is all the most learned and complete man knows at the summit of his development, above what he knew at birth. One's education may fit him for the greatest usefulness, or it may make him a skillful counterfeiter and a deceiver. At the first the child is taught most of what he learns directly by older persons. Later he is able to direct his own education and choose his helpers, whether persons, books, or objects. All that he knows, whether it be helpful or harmful to society, he has learned from some source, and constitutes his education. The important period for education is childhood and youth. This touches in a vital way one-third of the population at any given time, and all the people at some time. Whether the education given be helpful or whether it be harmful is of the most momentous importance.

True education is that which teaches one what will be a benefit to himself and others. False education is that which teaches one what will be an injury to himself or others. To teach a child to lie, to steal, to swear, to drink liquor or use tobacco, is to give him a false education. All those who by their habits or practices influence children to do these things are bad leaders, and are teaching false or pernicious education to childhood. The nation can not afford to allow one class of its citizens to profit by the ruin of another class, and especially the young and immature portion. This must condemn the whole liquor and tobacco business, as they can not be made profitable except by teaching the young to use these products to their hurt.

BUSINESS.

Business is that department of human activity which is occupied with the products and resources of the earth. It procures these in their native or crude state, prepares them for use, transports them to the place where they are needed, and sells them to the consumer. It concerns the buying, selling, or exchanging of any commodity or service. The great aim of true business is to produce a good, substantial article at a reasonable price, and distribute the proceeds fairly among all the producers.

The high aim of labor, or service, should be to do a

good, honest day's work for a reasonable price, and this aim applies to the ministers, the lawyers, and the doctors as well as to other kinds of labor, or service. The same principle ought to apply to the highest official at the top, and from that down to the boy beginning at the bottom of the scale.

True or honest business is one that works for the benefit of all concerned, whether producers or consumers. It aims to share or divide fairly the profits and also the losses due to natural and reasonable causes. False or dishonest business is one which by its nature works to the injury or loss of any persons concerned with it, whether producers or consumers. Liquor and tobacco are examples of false or dishonest business, as the consumer does not get value received for his money, and he is greatly injured by them.

SCIENCE.

Science is that department of human activity which seeks to know the absolute truth and the actual facts about everything and every principle. It seeks to know the relation of any one thing to all other things. Science asks the question: What is this? What is its use? Is it what it is supposed to be? Science can have no bias or prejudice; it must place the correct label on everything. False science is that which fails to discover the truth or to detect an error in any particular case or proposition.

The co-operation of the leaders and other persons engaged in these four lines of activity, namely: religion, education, business, and science—with each other and with the Creator is necessary for the highest well-being of humanity. In the past the failure of the leaders in these several departments to fully co-operate with each other and with the Creator has been the cause of most of the misfortune and misery that has come to humanity.

ESSENTIALS OF SELF-MASTERY SYSTEM

True education, true religion, true business, and true science work together for the good of man like the four fingers of a man's hand, like the four legs of a table, or like the four wheels of a wagon. If one of the four is defective, there is weakness, instability, or slow progress. In order to show the intimate relation which exists among these four great activities of life, I have called them together in council to consider three concrete cases. In these few words it is possible to give only a suggestion of the scope of each division. It is hoped that throughout the whole world the leaders and others engaged in these four departments will soon see the close relationship which exists among them, and that they will co-ordinate their forces and co-operate in all their labors for the common good of mankind.

We have here three cases: an idiot, an incurably insane man, and a degenerate. We will consider the first two together, and then take up the other case by itself.

"Education, can you do anything for these men?"

"No; neither of them can learn anything?"

"Science, can your department offer any cure for these men?"

"No; every known remedy and expedient has been tried, and both cases are hopeless."

"Business, what can you do for them?"

"I can build asylums and hire attendants to care for them, but it will not pay; they will simply suffer a few years longer, and there is no profit possible, but only loss."

Business, Education, and Science decide that it is better to give them an easy death at once, and if that were all there is in life, we would have to agree with this verdict. At this point Religion arises and says: "The command of our Creator and the law of right and justice forbid us to kill our fellow-man because he is unfortunate." Then turn-

31

ing to the others, Religion continues: "Science, you must find out what made this person an idiot, and what made that man insane, and discover means to prevent any more of our brothers and neighbors from such misfortunes. Business, you must furnish the means of caring for these, and also for making the investigation of the causes, and for preventing their continuance. Education, you stand near by and watch what Science does, and as soon as any fact is ascertained, you go and tell the whole world, and teach the people better ways. We are all disgraced by any human failure, and we must prevent its repetition. Business, you will need to furnish Education with the means necessary for this undertaking. The initial cost will be great, but it will pay in the end, as it will cut off those large expenses of caring for defectives. Now, I think, these cases are provided for."

Science now arises and requests permission to speak.

"Though I am perhaps the youngest member of this council, I must announce the fact that laws are written in the very nature of all created things, and I have no choice but to read these laws as I find the Creator has recorded them in the various branches of His works. I wish to ask each of you whether you will carry out whatever requirements my discoveries shall reveal as belonging to your several departments?"

Business replies: "That will have to depend on the cost. You might recommend fine fur and silk clothing for all the world, and I could not afford such luxuries, even if I should cut off all war and liquor bills."

Education replies: "I can not teach an old dog new tricks. If you require old people to change their ways and methods, it is beyond my power or sphere to carry out your recommendations."

Religion makes this reply: "Science, you will remember your youth, and that when you first stepped into the council you showed me very scant respect. Perhaps my representatives were too severe with you, but you must recall how you served your bread in the dough so many times that you spoiled our digestion, and we denounced you."

Science now acknowledged that he was impetuous and perhaps premature in some of his conclusions, but that he had kept his seat so long, he was impatient to get a hearing. At this point Business arose and stated that he had recently been working in co-operation with Science, and had found the partnership very advantageous in many ways; that Science had shown him how he could talk with his neighbor miles away over a wire, instead of going himself or sending a man with a message.

Seeing there were many delicate questions to settle, Business moved that the council retire into secret session and prepare a report for the public. This was done, and the result is the combined wisdom of the four departments of human activity. As Education is perhaps the oldest member of the council, and is respected by all, he was asked to make the report, and he gave the following:

"We have found that we must all work in harmony and co-operation if much is to be accomplished. After careful deliberation we have decided on the following acknowledgments and recommendations in respect to the several departments. Beginning with my own, I must report that there are many bad teachers who are demoralizing the world, yet whom I have been unable to dismiss. Some are teaching the boys to fight in war, and settle disputes by bloodshed and destruction of property. Some are teaching the children to drink liquor, use tobacco and other drugs, and also to follow other harmful habits, such as idleness and extravagance. Some are teaching them to get money, political offices, and other benefits dishonorably. I must ask the combined help of the other three departments in getting rid of these teachers of bad practices.

"Business allows me to report that his department has been too much absorbed in making money and in commercial progress, and has neglected the more vital interests of the very persons engaged in these enterprises. He requests the full co-operation of the other three departments in a better adjustment of business to the needs of men.

"We have decided that Science is to make a thorough investigation of any and all the ills of humanity, and that each department shall furnish any data within its knowledge that will aid Science in this work. Science must make sure of the facts and the truth before expecting his measures to be carried out on a large scale. When any fact is established, there shall be held a meeting of the council, and the four departments shall allot to each the part that falls to it in making any changes or improvements. Their united wisdom will decide on any measure, and their co-operative efforts will put the same into execution. Science promises to make an effort to allow none of his bread to be set on the table in the dough, but admits he has now and then in his employ a young enthusiast who is so anxious to announce some new discovery that he will rush into the dining-room and serve his bread on the table before it is ready even for the oven. Science also requests the full co-operation of the other departments in persuading the teachers of science to apply their wisdom and knowledge more thoroughly to eliminating from their own habits the use of liquor and those drugs which the department has condemned as being injurious to the young.

"Religion sees his mistake in not calling in the help of Science, Business, and Education to a much greater extent than he has done, in his work of leading men to do right in dealing with each other. The verdict of the other three departments is that Religion must cut loose from the dead weight of the past as found in faulty tradition, and move along with the times. Religion will need to kindly but firmly retire the high officials in positions of responsibility when they have passed their years of vigor and safe leadership. Only such persons as are young enough and vigorous enough to see mistakes and correct them are fit for high authority in religion or elsewhere. When one is too old to learn he is too old to rule others. Religion realizes the necessity of breaking with the false ideas of the past, and at the same time welcomes the day of greater harmony with the other departments."

SAVING A DEGENERATE.

We will now consider the case of the degenerate. Here is a man fifty years old. He is a bad man; he does not earn his living; he does not pay his debts; he uses tobacco; he gets drunk frequently, and when partly drunk, he may do almost anything. Now, can he be turned into a good neighbor and citizen? Can he be saved, or reformed, or whatever you choose to call it? "Education, what have you to say; can you do anything for him?"

"This man was born like thousands of others, but he had bad teachers to instruct him. His father and other neighbor men went fishing and hunting on Sundays, and he went with them and found bad company. They swore before him, and he learned to swear. They lied to him, and he tried to beat them at that. They gave him liquor, and he learned to drink. They smoked and chewed tobacco before him, and he thought that made a boy into a man, and began to use tobacco because the men used it. His mother did not use it, and they said a girl should not use tobacco; so his sister kept her mouth and breath clean. As a boy he was taught what was bad, and was not taught what was good. Now he is at the age where he will not learn better ways. He thinks he can not change, and he does not want to; hence I can do nothing for him."

"Business, you may speak. What can you do for him?"

"He knows better than he does. He has been told repeatedly that it does not pay to loaf about the saloons and spend his money there; but he does not heed. He has himself admitted that it is bad policy to get drunk and waste his money, instead of paying his debts; but he goes on in the same way. I have tried to convince him that it does not pay to live thus, and that there is a better way; but he pays no attention, and I can do no more for him."

"Science, can your department help this man?"

"I have showed him that alcohol is a poison, and not a food. I have showed him that tobacco is bad, even for an animal; that both of these interfere with health and comfort to himself and others; that they weaken the system and make it subject to disease, and unfit the body for the various strains liable to come upon it. I have proved to him that good food and water are better for the body than liquor and tobacco; but he does not heed. He is too old for much hope. A hardened steel bar can not be hammered and shaped into a useful tool; that must be done when it is hot—when it is young in its existence. At a sufficient heat it can be worked and shaped into any form. When it is old and rusty, like this man, there is no way to change it except to renew its youth by heat, so that it can be converted into another shape. If some power can renew this man's youth and bring him back to childhood, he can be regenerated, he can be made into a new, useful man. Science knows no other way. It is beyond the power of Education, Business, and Science to redeem him. They have tried repeatedly, and have saved so few that they find themselves utterly unable to cope with so great a problem. I refer his case to Religion."

"Religion, you have heard the discussion of this case; can you do anything for this man?"

"Science has given you the clue to his salvation. He can be reformed, made into a new, useful man, a good husband and neighbor, on one condition. As the cold steel must be returned to its childhood, so to speak, to a plastic nature, before it can be converted into another shape, so this man must be brought back to the state of childhood; that is, he must allow his mind to become like that of a little child, that can be molded by good influences and teachings. His mind must be changed; but no ordinary power can do that. His wife, his friends, and his neighbors have tried faithfully, and no change has taken place. I know of only one way. The Infinite Spirit that created this man's mind can even now renew and change this same mind if the man will come and allow it to be done. As the heat must enter the bar of steel to soften it, so must the Spirit of God enter the heart of this man to renew and convert it. He has said, 'Look unto Me, and be ye saved, all the ends of the earth.' That must include this man. Again, He has said, 'Ye will not come to Me, that ye might have life,' showing that He has given man the freedom of choice—he can come and get help, or he can refuse to come. He also says, 'Except ye be converted and become as little children, ye shall not enter the Kingdom of heaven.' This man's course, then, is plain: he must come to the Infinite Spirit and be made over into a new man. This is called conversion, or a new birth, and it is as truly scientific as it is to heat a spear in the fire and convert it into a pruning-hook. When an old stove, burned and used up, is again cast into the furnace, melted, and run into the molds to form a new stove, it is a new birth also. Both are scientific, both are according to reason, and both give hope to lives that are looking for better things. When this man's mind is changed, Education, Science, and Business can all unite with Religion in furthering his progress toward good citizenship."

Education, in summing up these cases, reports as follows:

"Business, Science, and Education are gratified to recognize the efficiency of Religion shown in converting a degenerate into a valued citizen. Each of these departments has come to see the imperative need of the help of Religion in forming and developing the minds and natures of all persons. Religion, being in close touch with the Creator and being concerned with the spiritual nature of man, can best change that nature and get him to adopt better ways.

"It is our unanimous verdict that, while the reformation of mature persons is desirable, yet it is very difficult, and is attended by many discouragements. The world must be reformed chiefly through work done with the children, both before and after their birth, and continued until they are mature and fully developed. When one generation of such human beings has been secured, the task of keeping humanity in close harmony and co-operation with each other and with the Creator will be easy and natural. The new, regenerated nature will rule to the end of time."

GENERAL PRINCIPLES.

Inasmuch as civilized humanity requires great labor and service for its support, every human being should do his part to earn his own living, and should take no more than his share of desirable things. If one fails to do his full part, he compels some one else to do his work; if he takes more than his share, he robs some one else. We must conclude then, that no power in heaven or earth can excuse any able-bodied person from doing his part or give him permission to take more than his share. It is impossible for one to become a self-master and meet all the requirements of a man without developing his powers and talents, and this he can do only by using them in the actual labors and contests of life. Jesus in His life as a model for us labored and earned His own living. He mastered Himself; He made use of His powers and talents, and brought them to their full development. Surely no human being, prince or peasant, can claim greater exemptions and privileges than the Son of God required as His due while He was among men.

EQUALITY.

Equality can not be worked as a principle in a system of growth and development; a man may not be equal to himself two days in succession. He should aim to excel his own yesterday, and to conquer his own to-morrow. The principle that must rule in the dealings of man with his fellow-man is that of fairness and justice to all. Men have different gifts and degrees of talent; some excel in business, some in invention, some in music and other specialties. The spirit of progress must allow each to advance as far as possible; but in moving forward he must not trample on the rights of others. The requirements for reaching the highest excellence in this life are identical with those for reaching the highest excellence in the life which is to come —there are not two lives, but one.

EVOLUTION.

If evolution means that a lower order can, unaided, evolve itself into a higher order, then it is irrational, and can not be applied to human beings as a working hypothesis in this world. The true principle of the creation of this world is growth and development, by each order reaching down and lifting up the one beneath it. The plant lifts up the inorganic, and organizes it into itself. The animal lifts up the plant, and organizes it into itself. Man lifts up the plant and the animal, and organizes them into himself, and uses them for his service. God reaches down and helps man up to become a co-worker with Him, and to shape himself according to the divine image.

The child, even after he is born, has no power to care for himself. He must be lifted up into the realm of maturity by older persons. Likewise the masses of the world must, through competent power and leadership, be lifted up into the realm of maturity sufficiently to make them masters of themselves. Only by this means can they protect themselves from bad leaders and guide the training and development of their children. The masses can not longer be held in ignorance and weakness by the hand of selfishness and despotism. They have learned something of their wrongs and their power. We who believe in right and justice must elevate them into intelligent, honest citizens, or the unprincipled agitators, who seek preferment at the cost of others, will, under some pretense of patriotism, lead them into excesses and violence. It is not necessary to have certain disastrous labor-wars repeated, but it will be possible if the masses are not protected from bad habits, bad morals, bad methods, and the influence of ignorant or unprincipled leaders.

AIM OF THE SELF-MASTERY SYSTEM.

The aim of the self-mastery system is to produce a race so well born and trained that every individual will police himself, support himself, and pension himself. The center of power and responsibility is to be placed within rather than outside of himself.

The introductory lesson in self-mastery is to teach the very young child to police himself by means of an outside authority that must be obeyed, and as rapidly as possible this authority is to be transferred to his own control. He must first learn to obey commands; later he learns the reason for obedience, and comes to realize that law and order are absolute in this world. He must be early taught to guard his own mouth, his hands, and his feet, that these should neither trespass on his own interests, nor on the rights of others. He must keep himself from being the servile tool of others for their sport or profit; he must learn not to allow himself to harm others, nor allow others to harm him.

There are those who tell us we should not say "do n't" to a child, and also that, if we forbid him to do any certain thing, that command makes him want to do it still more. It is only the ill-trained child that rebels against authority as a first impulse. The law of right and duty between man and man is as imperative as the law of life and death. There is an absolute *Do n't* in the foundation principles of all

40

nature. Experience and science find this word inscribed in fire, in water, in poison, in every disease-germ, and on the brink of every precipice. The child must have do n't said to him a great many times; in fact, until he has sense and understanding enough to take that duty into his own hands and say "do n't" to himself whenever he is tempted to wrong himself or others. At sixty years I consider Mr. Do n't one of my best servant-friends. He keeps me from trespassing on my own rights or the rights of others. I take him with me to the dining-room, to the playground, or any place of amusement, to church, and in all my travels, He protects me from the expensive merchant, the doctor, and the undertaker. Every one could greatly profit by employing Mr. Do n't as a chaperon, and no well-trained person could object to such companionship. Most of the excellent people of this world are such because very early in life they locked arms with Mr. Do on one side and Mr. Do n't on the other, and thus supported they walked up to an eminence of merit.

The final purpose of the whole self-mastery system is to make every person in a large degree self-governing, self-inspiring, self-directing, and complete.

TESTS OF THE SELF-MASTERY SYSTEM.

As scientists test various articles of food to ascertain their purity, or what valuable elements they may possess, so the purpose of these tests is to detect the presence or the absence of any helpful or harmful principle, and to discover the true and the false wherever they may be found. As a means of examining any institution, custom, or principle, personify it, and treat it as an individual doing all that that particular idea or custom is responsible for.

General Test.—What is wrong with the world? What is wrong with the individual? What is wrong with myself? Who is to blame? What is the remedy?

Justice Test.—To be used in examining any measure, policy, or law. Is it just to every one, tending to make the people honest, free, and able to care for themselves; or does it give an unfair advantage to a few powerful rulers or bosses, making the masses dependent and subject to them?

Quadruple Test.—This applies to the fitness of a person for any position of trust or responsibility:

1. Intelligent. Has he the required knowledge for the position?
2. Capable. Is he able to do what the position requires?
3. Honest. Will he do not less than his part of the work or service, nor take more than his share of the proceeds, whether money, honor, or privilege?
4. Free. Is he at liberty to perform all the duties of the position, and not bound by prejudice, tradition, or party?

Companion Test.—Is he a good companion? Is he a good neighbor? Is he a good partner?

Companion and neighbor concern more directly the spiritual and social side of man. Partner touches every business transaction between man and man. The two persons may be associated in the same business, or as buyer and seller, doctor and patient, lawyer and client, teacher and pupil; or in any act of life in which two persons exchange or share some commodity or service. No man has any right to be a bad or unfair partner simply because his fellow-man is in his power.

Triple Test of Science, Religion, and Business.

This test is applied to things, methods, and principles. Science asks: What is it? Is it true? Is it genuine? Is it what it is represented to be?

Religion asks: Is it right toward God? Is it right toward my fellow-man? Is it right toward myself? Does it keep the Golden Rule?

Business asks: Will it pay? Is it the best way? Is there no better way?

Tendency Test.—Does it tend in the direction of the best people, toward God, and the greatest ultimate gain?

Does it tend in the direction away from God, toward the worst people, and the greatest ultimate loss?

THE TWO SYSTEMS OF MASTERY.

We are led to see that two systems of life and government were offered to man in the beginning.

God gave man the mastery of self, the true system which is inherent in His own being, and hence suited to man made in the divine image. It includes all that is good and profitable in developing the human race.

Satan gave man the false system, the mastery of others. For one person to make himself master of another person is in direct disobedience and defiance of the truth, and is contrary to the very nature of God and of man made in the image of God.

God's system was: Master and develop yourself; subdue the earth, and have dominion over all created things beneath you. God has never sought to master men, but to make them strong and honest, in order that they might be trusted to govern themselves.

Satan's system was: Master your fellow-men; compel them to serve you, to subdue the earth, and to bring you its treasures. Satan seeks to master men and to weaken them through indulgence, in order that he may rule them.

God's system meant the freedom of all mankind through the knowledge and practice of the truth, and through the right dealing of each man with his fellow-man. God offered His system to man in the beginning, and a few have been found all along the ages who have accepted and followed His plan.

Satan's system meant the bondage of all, through wrong and unfair dealing between man and his fellow-man. Satan

43

offered his system, and it was accepted by the few strong ones desirous of ruling others. They enforced it on the multitude, and the disasters of humanity have come through that bad method. Satan offered his system to Jesus, but it was rejected, because Jesus did not seek to rule the world, or the kingdoms of the world, but to teach and prepare the people and the kingdoms to rule themselves.

COMPARATIVE COST OF THE MASTERY-OF-SELF AND THE MASTERY-OF-OTHERS.

Who pays the cost? The mastery-of-self is very economical, and the cost is paid by each one for himself. God is its Author and the Great Self-master. Of His own, He gave the world with all its wealth; He gave man life and wonderful talents; He gave prophets and teachers to guide man, and, greatest of all, He gave His Son to instruct and redeem mankind. Christ gave of His own all that Divinity prized most: love, service, and sacrifice. At last, by His resurrection, He gave man the proof of His power over death, and with it the evidence of man's immortality. From first to last in God's system of self-mastery, each gives what is his own; each pays the cost of all he seeks to get with his own; and thus each becomes free and independent of everything but the law of righteousness.

Compare this now with the mastery-of-others system. Call its author Satan, or Evil, or what you will, it is antagonistic to God, and it is the embodiment of opposition and disobedience to Him. While the mastery-of-self is economical and pays its own cost, the mastery-of-others is frightfully expensive, and the cost is paid by others. The very few riot in luxuries that are bought by the blood and treasure of the vast multitude. The cost of war, crime, persecution, and oppression is the penalty paid for following the false system.

In the realm of war, note the history of Napoleon. It

would stagger the imagination to count the cost of placing that man on the throne of France, and of sending him to St. Helena. The homes destroyed, the cities burned, the provinces devastated, the myriads of lives sacrificed—the value of all these was the price paid by others in the attempt of one monster to rule his fellow-men by a false principle.

Mohammed was another who sought to bring the whole world under his control and make others pay the cost. Measure the vices and degradation of Mohammedanism from its founder to the present time, and you will measure simply one item of the world's misery caused by following a false system.

The popes of Rome for many centuries have been trying to buy for themselves the mastery of the political and religious world. The cost has all been paid by others, and it has been ruinous in its magnitude. The religious wars, the Inquisition, the loss of freedom to the people, the sacrifice of the liberties of the priesthood and the monastic orders, all these are part of the price paid by one succession of men who used a pernicious system in an attempt to rule others.

It would have been more Christ-like, and infinitely better, to have sent forth those men and women, equipped with the open Bible and with the freedom of the truth, to make the remotest child of the earth an intelligent master of himself. If that line of popes had first mastered themselves after the pattern of the Great Teacher, and then had become leaders of men, instead of trying to make themselves masters of men, they would have won eternal honors, and the world would have become a Garden of the Lord before this. Many of them were brave and heroic men, but they labored to establish a false system, hence its cost and failure. Jesus said: "If any man will come after Me, let him deny himself—master himself—take up his cross, and follow Me." Again He said: "Ye shall know the truth and the truth shall make you free."

By following the right system, we who know the truth can with reasonable effort and expenditure place it within reach of the whole world. There is not one trace of malice or of destructiveness in God's system of self-government; its establishment carries with it only love and light, peace and good will among universal humanity.

CHAPTER II

SELF-MASTERY OF MEN

BY self-mastery, I mean the control and management of myself in all matters pertaining to my own personal movements and desires. It includes the control and service of the various resources of the earth, understood in their fuller sense. I am composed of body and spirit. These two, so far as this world is concerned, are inseparably bound together; separated, both disappear. In the beginning, spirit and body are crude in the extreme. Both grow together in an apparent and somewhat serious rivalry and contest. Unaided, a savage is the result. With proper guidance on the part of parents and older persons, the body and spirit of the child develop together, each keeping its own place. This means a life partnership of the closest and most harmonious friendship and co-operation of the two. The result is a wonderful product, a complete man or woman, made in the image of God.

The master of a violin must be able to bring out all of its possibilities as a musical instrument. The master of himself must bring out of himself all his possibilities as a human being. As man is several years old, and well started in some direction before he even knows he is going anywhere, it is plain that some one else has a grave responsibility for his right starting. Even in a horse-race it is conceded that each should have a fair chance to start, and I claim as much for every child. Others must provide for him parentage and birth, food, shelter, and clothing for his body, until he is able to care for himself. For his spirit or mind he must have a teacher, a model, and companionship to guide and afford him an example of conduct.

SELF-MASTERY OF MEN AND NATIONS

Self-mastery means to master and develop one's self and the resources and products of the earth, and help others to do the same. I include the helping of others, because the person who only takes care of himself has not paid back the help he received before he could help himself, and because civilization binds people together in mutual helpfulness.

WHAT SELF-MASTERY MEANS TO ME.

I can best explain this term by giving my own experience. I claim perfection in no line, but a degree of success that brings a large return for the investment, and proves the correctness of the system. I divide myself by a line just above my mouth; all above that line must be master, and all below must be servant, and these two co-operate. I will not take any food or drink that forms a habit; everything put into my mouth can find a substitute. I can go without bread, meat, potatoes, etc., taking the substitutes that people of different parts of the world use. We need variety of cereals, vegetables and fruits, but these do not form habits. These are foods, not stimulants; one can be substituted for the other in a little time. I used coffee for years, but finding myself with a headache without it, we parted company; coffee can not be my master. Of course I do not use liquor, tobacco, or any drugs. I like various games, but will not play those that fascinate me or others. I want games that tire or satisfy me when I have played long enough. Water satisfies one when he has had enough, wholesome games do the same. Alcoholic drinks lead to excess, so does gambling, hence the self-master lets them alone, if not for his own sake, for those more easily led than he. A self-master can not allow himself to be used as a stool-pigeon to lead others into traps. Self-mastery makes a man master of his own desires and wants. He will not be like the tortoise in the fable, that wanted to fly, and persuaded the eagle to carry him up in the air and let him drop. It must make one satisfied with what is possible at any given time

48

or place; more than this, it must make one satisfied with what is best.

CARE OF THE BODY.

A man having to cross a continent on one horse, riding over plain and mountain, fording rivers, wading in mud, breaking through snowdrifts and enduring the extremes of heat and cold, must do two things. First, he must study the horse's nature and possibilities; second, he must obey those laws of horse nature that preserve its powers. The horse is his servant and friend. He must become the master of that horse in the sense of making him very useful. So must man do with his own body, which is his friend and servant. My body must last through the journey of life. I do not ride a lame horse; he may fail me in a critical moment. I will not lend or hire my horse to a foolish or bad driver. After he has done a day's work, no one shall have him for a midnight frolic. So with my body, ten or eleven o'clock at night is late enough for any frolic. It is the fool's fun that comes after that.

I am spirit and animal. I will not let my animal injure or destroy himself. I will not let him eat himself sick, drink himself drunk, or go capering on the brink of a precipice. My body is my donkey that carries me and all my possessions. Some call the donkey stupid, he has far more sense than the man who drinks booze or uses tobacco. Give him all the liberty of the world and he will not harm himself.

I profit greatly by applying the principles of self-mastery every day; without them all would be changed. It would cost me more than I could spend in this work, and perhaps so much as to turn me aside from a great purpose. These principles give me great freedom; they give me the wings of a bird to fly above the bogs, creeks and marshes. When God can trust me with more liberty, it may be placed within my reach. Let me quote directly from my notes of travel:

"Florence, Italy, April 18, 1912. I am up at 5.20, eager

to study Italian. I believe my zeal in studying French, Italian, and Spanish at sixty is partly due to the scientific physical fact of simple food and fresh air, no tobacco, spirits, tea, coffee or other stimulants. I take no food or drink that clogs the system and clouds the spirit. This mode of life puts the work of the engine as the great aim of existence, instead of the consumption of fuel, as the high liver seems to do. To prepare the fuel so the furnace would consume a great deal would be like employing a fancy cook to enable me to eat more after I had eaten enough.

"Oh, how I enjoy my freedom! My wife and I stood near the old monastery at the summit of Fiesole heights, enjoying the grand view of the valley of the Arno and Florence. In extensive travel, I have seen but few to equal it. I said to my wife: 'I do not know any one, and in all the history I have read I do not recall any one so free as I am. For a few cents I can buy a sufficient meal, and sitting on a little terrace wall with my companion for life and travel, I can eat it while historic old Florence lies at my feet.' We had a very simple meal of bread and butter with fruit and some nuts, and later I took a drink at the public fountain from my hand. My great freedom at the present time lies in the fact of health, strength, and the wealth that come from being entirely satisfied with the plain things of life that are easily provided. We divide both the great and small benefits; I should feel mean to take more than my share. It would mar the happiness of both if I should make myself vile with tobacco, and compel my wife to breathe the smoke and get nothing out of her share of the money thus spent. I believe God's plan is that all people should reach a period in life where they can nearly have their own way and do as they like. This is neither reasonable nor possible until one has learned self-mastery. One must be satisfied with plain food, clothing and shelter. One must prefer to wait on himself, and give others as little trouble as possible. He must find more pleasure in giving to others and helping them, than in receiving from them. He must find more joy in being fair and honest with his life companion, than in any course of selfishness and indifference to the other's rights. To be too lazy or too incompetent to care for one's self, is no preparation for a life of full satisfaction and freedom. Servants who do everything in the right time and manner are not standing in the markets to be hired. If you want such a one, you must train him. To be a successful teacher, you must begin with yourself. By the time you have succeeded to your hearts' content with this first pupil, you will likely say, either "I have had such a time training one servant I do not care to take another," or you will say, "I have now a good trained servant, and we two will stay together for life."

The self-master must be a true scientist. He must insist on the verity of things, and the genuineness of what he accepts—whitewash and veneer are all right in their place, but they must pass for what they are. He must be a good business man, he must not pay more for a thing than it is worth. He must be able to discern future values and remember that all values can not be expressed by the $ sign. Character, integrity, and faithfulness, which can neither be boxed nor crated, have a commercial value that no good business man will overlook.

RESPECT FOR OTHERS' RIGHTS.

I must require myself to be respectful to another person's worship, whether he be Roman, Hebrew, or idolater. I would not be rude to one who ignorantly worshiped his hoe, or anything else; I would like, however, to teach him better. The one who seems to worship himself, tests my code of politeness the worst.

A large faith in God and humanity and a love for both are necessary for self-mastery. Without these, my own desire and natural energy in caring for myself would overreach my judgment and lead me to injure myself and dishonor myself. I have known cases of this kind. Some persons, feeling they are paying too much for their board, eat to their injury to get their money's worth. Some take trouble to waste a little, or at least they are careless and add to the expense, and thus keep prices up. Both are degrading, for it is yielding to a low impulse to get even with one we think unjust. I knew a student who left his coat off in his room, and kept his fire too hot to be comfortable, to get the worth of his board money. I once boarded at a students' club, where economy expected each of us to take but one apple at dinner, as this fruit was expensive at that time. There was but one person, I believe, who offended in this matter. This one always came promptly, ate one apple quickly before dinner, another just after, and frequently took a third as he left the table, before most of us had finished. There was a degree of courtesy among those students that would allow that thing without audible protest, but his conduct is the most vivid remembrance I have of that man, and I doubt not others of the club remember the same fact. This principle holds in business where men take more than their share of the profits. They rob others, and occasionally load themselves down with riches that reduce them to the level of a mere toiling machine. They lose the joy of wealth, in the loss of respect for humanity by their own crookedness. A man who knows himself to need watching, is likely to overdo his watchfulness of others in protecting himself.

A self-master must be able to speak to himself with authority and say, "Now you have eaten enough, let that tempting dish alone." Also there are times when he must say, "Now that is good food, you have to work, you must eat, you must believe it is good enough. Thousands of other persons are content with it, and you must be." I have proved this to be possible, both when I lacked appetite and when the fare was too plain. In my wide travels it has happened that, by chance, I saw too much in the kitchen. I do not care to enter into details here; sometimes ignorance is not only pardonable but desirable.

That man is fortunate who can compel obedience when he says to himself, "You have money enough, you have your share, let some one else have a chance." It is especially sad to see an old man use unfair means to keep young men from starting in business, when he ought to encourage them. Those who have helped the young to start, instead of hindering them, tells us it pays in the end. I do not believe a strong, vigorous nature, such as can succeed in business, can compel himself to do the generous act without the aid given him by his belief in God and humanity. To get aid in this way is not a mark of weakness, but of strength—a mastery over a giant, himself. As well obtain aid thus to get over one's own inward difficulties, as to use the aid of a boat in crossing a stream. The boat is servant, not master. One's respect for his fellows serves him and honors him too. Self-love and self-interest are so prone to go too far and injure their owner that they need strong chains to hold them within bounds. It is like keeping a tiger for a watch-dog, there is danger of his injuring his master. Self-love and self-interest are very good watch-dogs, but better not have them too large and fierce. Napoleon I. made that blunder, and his self-love and self-interest landed him in St. Helena. A proper regard for the rights of his wife, for his country, and for the rest of Europe would likely have kept him on the throne of France. What untold atrocities and barbarities would thus have been spared to the world, and especially to Europe! The disaster wrought by the selfishness and conceit of that one man is utterly beyond computation. He has been called a great man, and his name has been flaunted in the face of the youth as a hero. I believe the better and final verdict of history will be that he was a monster of selfishness. His infidelity to his wife and to other women, and his disregard of everybody's rights,

53

make him such a monster. Some of the modern Napoleons of finance, sometimes called Captains of Industry, deserve rather the title of "Commercial Bandit."

I have never experienced the sensations of those who command large forces of men or money. That is the privilege of the few. I have, however, many times tasted the joy of command over circumstances, and the powers and forces within me. This joy is new every morning. It comes as I breathe the air of Alps or Appenines, and drink their snow-melted waters. It comes as I walk beneath the palms of the tropics, brush the dew from the heather of Ireland, or breathe the perfume of the pines of Norway. I have this joy also, that no curses of the conquered nor groans of the dying torture my ear. Some in many lands say, as I talk with them and then go on my way with my luggage in my own hand, "There goes a foreigner and a stranger who feels with us who toil. He calls us his neighbors and treats us as such." The world has room for fifteen hundred million such conquerors, each one a self-master.

A fawning courtier said to Philip II of Spain, when he was but five years old, as he looked down on the multitude from the palace, "You own all those people." His after life and history show that this was a pernicious falsehood to teach the child. Rather he should have been told: "Even your clothes were earned and are owned by some one else, but they are freely furnished you while you are too young to earn them. Your first duty is to learn to serve yourself, to master yourself, and the circumstances about you. You are to serve these people for their good. If you do this, the people will not forget to honor you."

God's condition of personal content and happiness requires one to do more than his share of the hard work of the world, and receive for it less than he has truly earned. This excess means progress. Exactly balanced accounts would mean stagnation, or even decay. What one does is apt to look larger to himself than to others. What he receives is apt to look smaller to him than to others. If every person could be put on canvas in two pictures, the one how big he looks to himself, and the other how big he looks to the world, would there not be some odd contrasts! It might require a large canvas in one case, and a strong microscope in the other to make both plain.

Discussing the question of taking third class passage on a certain steamer, I am asked, "Is there a steerage also?" The import of the question is, "Is there a still lower class to take the least desirable persons away from my presence?" My reply is, "I have no right to fix for myself this condition of comfort, that some one else must have less than I have." There is far too much of that spirit in human make-up. Some persons want to travel first class and have others in the second or third class for the sake of contrast. It is a bad spirit that seeks to rise by putting some one else down. That was not the Master's way. It is not even the way a bird rises in the air. He spreads his own wings and rises by mastering himself and the elements. If we who have had better chances than those in the steerage, do not like their company nor their accommodations, it is in our power to improve both to the degree of making them tolerable to us. Sometimes the steerage people are crowded because the big ones with their suites of rooms take more than their share of the space. Shame on the man or woman who has no other claim to distinction except the money to buy new clothes frequently, and then to demand some freak mark on them to show they are the latest style. They thus make young men and women, doing honest work on small wages, ashamed of good clothes simply because they are a little out of style. This very thing leads many young persons into vice, immorality and crime. Many of these rich and stylishly dressed people are parasites, and never even earned their own living. They are corrupting the young, by their bad example, with other people's money. There is an element which says, "Take the money away from the rich and extravagant by force." That would be criminal; two crimes do not neutralize each other. The remedy is to teach the young better ways. We can remedy many ills by a good healthy public sentiment. If certain people were made to feel they were not envied, but despised for their prodigal waste of the earth's products that God meant for all, they would soon change. Many of them could thus be transformed into good, desirable citizens.

THE MASTERY OF MONEY.

One very important field of conquest is the mastery of money. I have no war against money or wealth; both are necessary, and are the results of labor and service applied to God's gifts of material. *Neither is there any question of equality of wealth among people*—talent to handle money varies as other special talents do. The presence of paupers and of multi-millionaires, however, shows great faults somewhere. There is urgent need of instruction in the right use of money, and of a strong sentiment to make all men honest and public-spirited so that they will be fair in the distribution of the profits from business and in grasping the world's natural resources.

Let me now give the substance of the teaching of my home and of later experience in this matter. It is my purpose here to combine the wisdom of religion, education, business, and science. I shall personify this knowledge, to help others grasp the true nature and use of money, and better appreciate its value. Mr. Money is not afraid to stand up in a strong light before a mirror and look at himself. He is willing to be examined by any and all experts by means of the most searching tests. They may use accurate scales, the microscope, or acids; he will stand the triple test of science, business and religion. Like religion, he is not responsible for any counterfeits; they must stand on their own merits.

MY FATHER INTRODUCES ME TO A GOOD FRIEND.

"My son, I introduce you to an old friend and servant of the family. You will need to get well acquainted with him, and learn how to get along with him. He is very obedient and useful in the hands of a master, but he has great power for harm if he is wrongly used. If he harms you, after you have had a chance to know his powers and possibilities, it is your own fault. Treat him well and he will serve you; honor him and he will honor you; dishonor him and he will dishonor you, and very likely leave you. There is no telling to what degree of misery and wretchedness you may come if he should desert you, or you should desert him. Bear in mind, however, that you must be the master, not he. Also remember always and everywhere, the master and servant are friends. If each person performs his part, knows his place, and is honest and true to himself and to his Maker, all goes well. You two had better sit down and have a talk, and get acquainted with each other. Mr. Money has traveled very extensively, has moved in the best society, and also in the worst. He was given a duty to perform for men in the education and happiness of the race. Wherever that duty called him, he has gone and has done his part. He is not to blame for the bad reputation some people have given him. Like some persons, his reputation has suffered from the acts of others. They were weak and bad, and have taken him with them into all sorts of sin and folly, and then they have laid the blame on him. If a man uses his hands to cut off his toes, he must not blame his hands or the ax, but himself. My son, I introduce you to your friend and servant, Mr. Gold Dollar Money."

"Good morning, Mr. Money, I am glad to meet you; I trust we shall always be friends. I like true friends, and I am trying to get more of them. We do not call anybody servant in our house, except with the thought of honor and respect; we try to serve God, ourselves, and each other. Father says you have traveled very extensively, that you have had great opportunities to learn and to know the world. I have wanted to travel and see the world ever since I began to study geography. Do tell me about yourself. Where do you come from, and what have you seen in your travels? I hope you may help me to travel some time. I am surely very glad to have so valuable and experienced a friend."

"My young friend, I am very glad to meet you and to serve you to the best of my ability. I trust our associations will be mutually helpful. Your parents are both old friends of mine; they have always considered me as one of the family, and have neither abused nor dishonored me. I am really an agent representing the firm of Service, Labor & Company, a firm of very wide experience. Like many other firms, it was very small at first, but now is very large and influential. As to my origin, you and I have the same Creator. God made me and put me away for safekeeping until I was needed. Some other metals and minerals, such as iron and coal, He made in very large quantities, and put on the surface or near it where they were easily found. He gave me a different work to do, made me rare and placed me where men have to dig and work hard to get me. You have heard me called by all sorts of names, clean and pure, and vile and filthy, by turns. I have been praised and honored as the divine and good, and I have been maligned and had all sorts of blame laid upon me. Everybody is after me; some treat me well and I stay with them; some treat me shamefully and I leave them. Some have boasted, and claimed to be very distinguished because they have had me in their service. Some have taken vows of poverty and would not have me with them, and then they go around begging their bread from my friends who treat me better. Some persons make me into rings for their ears, fingers and noses, crowns for their heads, and chains for their necks, and then they strut around like a peacock with his tail spread, with this difference—the peacock wears his own fineries, these people boast themselves in borrowed garments.

"I have been greatly misunderstood by the world, good and bad. The fact is, I am one of God's servants and have an individual duty to Him. I must be true to myself, and to my mission, somewhat like a human being. If I am gold in the hands of a saint, I must be gold in the hands of a sinner; I owe this to myself and to my Maker. I am the same lying in the mud as when worn as an ornament by a king. If I were not so, I would be of no use.

"If you honor me, I will honor you in return. If you trade me off for some worthless thing, or something that is bad, such as liquor, tobacco or vice, you dishonor me and I will be a curse to you. If you send me to do any mean, disgraceful work, I will leave you, and the blame and the penalty will finally fall on yourself and others. People will reject you and put you out, but they will welcome me back at the mere sight of me. If from being in dirty hands, I am dirty and unattractive on the outside, they will always look below the surface with me, but not always the same with you. Even when my representative, Mr. Paper Money, goes in my place, they always welcome him back from anywhere. Though he is ragged and dirty, if there is enough of him left, so they can recognize his face, they receive him. They accept him from black, yellow or white people. No race or color mark counts against the Money family.

"People may call me evil names, but they do not mean it. You must judge a man by his conduct, not by his words, if the two do not agree. They say the fool and his money are soon parted, and then after the separation everybody runs after the money, but nobody cares for the society of the fool. If they flattered and fawned on him before, it is plain now that his worth lay in his money and not in himself. I do not like a fool's company. I would never stay with one at all if it were not that he has some sensible friend in the house who does not disgrace me. You know some rich men raise their children as fools, and then even after they are grown up, they have to employ some prudent person to stay in the house and look after me or I would leave them. The fault was that the parents gave too much of their time and attention to me and to enjoying themselves, and too little to their own children. They say I am a good servant, but a bad master. The same is said of fire and water; both are true. Gold, fire, water, and all other elements and forces were given each its place in the service of God and man. Where we cause any serious discord in the affairs of men, it is because they have failed to use their intelligence to the best account. We are the friends of man, and God has given us our fields of service which we can not desert. You fill your place as faithfully as we do ours, and you will help and not hinder the cause of progress."

"Thank you, Mr. Money, for your interesting and instructive history. I see you are a valuable friend, and I shall do my best to honor you, by never sending you on any disgraceful errands. I will make this agreement with you. You are never to part from me without leaving a good substitute in your place; some one who for that particular occasion can serve me better than you can. When I need to call for the help of some other friend such as bread or books, fuel or railroad tickets, I shall have to send you after them. I will never send you after any booze, and very rarely after any foolishness."

"Very well, young man, stand by your part of the contract, and I will stand by mine."

I wish it were possible in a few words to tell all the young people of the world what an excellent servant-friend money is. I take off my hat in respect to the great business integrity of the civilized world in the matter of money, as I have been so greatly aided by it in my travels in foreign lands. It strengthens my faith in God and humanity enormously, and I see that ere long the time will come when, as a gold coin is now the standard of value in business, so the personal Christ will become the standard and measure of a man the world around.

CHAPTER III

THE INDIVIDUAL AND SELF-MASTERY

GOD is the most perfect individual possible. He is a distinct entity. He can not be confused with others. Though God is a perfect individual, He was not satisfied to remain alone, nor was He content simply with the creation of the universe and the lower forms of life. This means a great degree of personal responsibility for each individual man and woman.

Man is a distinct individual; he can not cross with any animal. He is born as if the only one and dies as if alone. He can live alone if others will let him, but he is liable to become helpless and dependent. This fact proves that man's independence and individuality are limited to their definite spheres. Like the two wheels of a cart, each has its part to perform, but to accomplish the work of the cart combination is necessary; they must co-operate.

Man must make his own child so strong in body and spirit that he will give up his life before he will yield to grievous sin. His child must become strong and good enough to walk with God, and have God satisfied with his company. Christ walked with His disciples, and all went well while they were willing to learn and try to keep step with Him. The crowds followed Him and accepted His food and other miracles, the Pharisees and scribes tried to direct His plans, and a rupture followed. In all co-operation the finite must conform to the infinite, and not the reverse.

Each individual must have knowledge and the right to come directly to God in the development and duties of his personality. God has made the way, and man must teach every child to find and use it for himself. This is a privilege and duty which he owes to God, to himself, and to his neighbors. Any person who sets himself up as a toll-gate between God and His children is an enemy to both. No person has the right to stand between any child and God except as a light to guide, or a finger-post to point the way.

The smallest individual or unit has rights and duties that can not be delegated to others. An individual stone has its identity, yet it allows itself to become merged into a larger unit such as a house or wall. So man must allow his individual to be merged into the larger unit of the family, the nation, and the world. It is the duty of every human unit to become a part of larger benevolent units such as Christian work requires, but not in an army for oppression or plunder, nor in any combination for dishonest or fraudulent purposes. A rope of sand and a heap of fiber are neutral factors. As the grains of sand are united by cement, and the fibers of the rope by twisting, so men must be held together by a combining element of common interest.

Man tries to reproduce himself in an automatic machine. He has accomplished much, but finds his limitations, as the thing made can never equal its maker; he could not give it life and will power. What would happen if he could? The same that happens between man and his Maker now—the machine would defy its maker and rebel against him until it learned better. We must believe man's rebellion is caused by his lack of training and knowledge, as a rational being will choose the best of several courses when he knows them and is master of himself. Men are coming to understand God better, and see that He does not need servants to bring Him some object, but that He desires companionship in love and in His work for the race. Man can not create anything, but he can so transform material that it very closely resembles creating. Man would not be satisfied with his machines, however perfect; he would want to talk and think with his own, and God has provided for this. A pair, one man and one woman, may unite and several children of their own flesh and blood are within their power. These offspring share the color and characteristics of their parents, and while young they are so immature and plastic that the parents can teach them their language, guide their thoughts, and shape their lives. Thus the parents lead their children on to maturity with God's help, and at last the children may care for the aged parents, and train successors to themselves. The children of other parents may be adopted and become as one's own, thus proving the common parentage of all mankind, and also that all can live as one great family. Is anything in the range of thought more complete and excellent than this?

Serving one's self.—The individual needs to be taught the honor and dignity of all useful work. No human being has any right to ask or hire another to do for him what he would be ashamed to do for himself. It does not matter whether it be regarded as a menial task such as to scrub a floor or wash one's clothes; or whether it be to wreck a bank, sell liquor, or become an agent for some other crime. Such an idea as a "servant class" is preposterous, and an enemy of self-mastery and individual development. In the growth of each there is a period of service in simpler things, then that of a more difficult nature. God intended each individual to wait on himself where this is possible, and not to keep slaves or servants. He may have helpers in anything, and to any extent needed, but this fixes no rank. Christ Himself served others and lost no dignity, but gained thereby. No animal, useful to man, lives on the blood of others; beasts and birds of prey are of no further use than their skins or plumage.

FAITH HEALING AND INDIVIDUAL PRAYERS.

I heard an address at the cathedral in Algiers by the Chanoine Ballon to a large audience of men. He is a very gifted orator and speaks French so that it sounds like music.

He spoke half an hour to a rapt congregation, mostly in defense of miraculous healing, and especially of the claims put forth for the Grotto of Lourdes. He attacked all opponents of those claims. He said: 'Cures are genuine, instantaneous and complete. Scientists find the plague in rats and prevent the spread of the disease. They affect material by material; Lourdes cures without material.' My reply and application is this: 'Whatever the Church at Lourdes may do, its cures are very limited and hard to reach. It would seem better for all cures to be conducted on a larger and more scientific scale by using any available means, and by having it done at home—sick people are in no condition to take long journeys. If God cures through the agency of Lourdes, how is it to be reconciled with His wisdom and His individual care of men? I reply, 'The individual is so important in God's plan and promise that at times He hears the prayer and heals the patient, even though some one may take advantage of these circumstances for selfish purposes, or even to propagate a fraud and make money. The Church, the Mormons, Dowie, and others have been accused of doing this. Would you let your child drown when he had fallen into the water, simply because your enemy would cling to his clothes and thus be rescued? Would you let your child starve rather than have some enemy share his food for a brief time? Your duty and care for your individual child would be the mastering motive in spite of all else, and you would help both to save your child. So with God, for He sends rain on the just and the unjust.

Individual persons, like individual telephone poles, must be able to support themselves and each help his neighbor on either side. A broken pole that hangs on the wires may ruin the line; such poles are soon removed under good management. The same principle holds with persons, and the one who hangs as a dead weight on his neighbors is a menace to the community. Each person should feel that it is an honor to support himself and help his neighbor, and that it is a disgrace to hang as a dead weight on others and be supported by them. Society has far too many rotten telephone poles, from the ranks of the haughty and wealthy beggar down to the poor beggar and tramp. The rich beggar riding in an expensive auto is far more contemptible than the wayside tramp, and he exerts a more baneful influence on the young.

It is a good thing for one to stand off at a little distance and look at himself occasionally. I like to think of myself as the man who will not waste money on himself or any one else; who will not be a slave to his gullet or any other part of his body; whose head must rule, and even the better part of that. The head is virtually the individual of the body, the gullet is a sort of superintendent of the stomach and digestive system, and the reproductive organs are superintendents of race continuance, having an important function touching the virility and self-assertion of the whole man. The gullet and reproductive organs are so strong they are prone to overreach their duties, and work ruin to the man. They are good servants if the head keeps them in their true places and does not allow them to do any bossing.

The individual can not delegate his own peculiar duties to others. It is plain that the body must eat, sleep, and rest for itself, if it is to grow or even live. This proves that the spirit also has independent duties necessary to its life and growth. The spirit must come in contact with the mind and person of God its Maker; it must think of Him and receive inspiration and growth from Him. My spirit and body take counsel together in all things. The spirit must not keep the body at work too long without rest, nor allow too much idleness. I have many times been tired in my study and felt like lying down, but my spirit told me to go out and exercise in the open air. The spirit must not allow the body to eat or drink to its own hurt. The body must not load the stomach so as to drown and deaden the spirit. Both meet in counsel, but the spirit must rule. The spirit can train the body to many changes by degrees. It must train all heads of departments, such as the mouth, the eyes, the hands, and brain, in rigid service to the higher nature. The great end of this structure, called man, is to become a complete, individual master of itself, and its further development.

THE HUMAN FAMILY AS AN INDIVIDUAL.

As the body can not grow by consuming itself—by one part living on another—so the individual race must not consume itself. The law of growth for this world is that each order shall grow by reorganizing the lower into itself. The plant reorganizes the soil, the animal feeds on the plant, and man consumes both plants and animals in his growth.

The greatest blunder of the present is for one part of the race to cheat and plunder another part, that is an attempt to get what another has earned, while giving no equivalent for it; that is communal suicide. It must become the rule to give as much for service and commoditites as is consistent with that side of the bargain; and to give as much of service and of wares as that side will allow. In short, we ought to pay the largest price we can afford, and give as much for the price as we can afford. There is a tradition that a king should be generous whether he buys or sells— in buying he must give a good price, in selling he must give good measure. The self-mastered individual must be a king in these things. There is an element and ideal in kingship that should be preserved, and used liberally as an ingredient in the future race when every man shall be king of himself and his sphere of action. That was the Great Teacher's way and His example to men. His rule was, never destroy but transform; never fraud and robbery, but fair and honest exchange.

THE MOB SPIRIT.

The crime of the mob is that the individual is lost in the crowd. It is a kind of madness that runs away with reason and does foolish and criminal things. The mob spirit—the extinction of the individual in the crowd—is the crime of nations in war, and of smaller groups in society, in false religions, in fashion, and in political parties and corporations. The separate individuals would not do what the combined individuals do where each shirks his duty.

For a frolic, people sometimes assume a degree of savagery, put on grotesque masks to hide their faces, and show rudeness not their wont when unmasked. Officers and men in armies and corporations hide behind the "army" or the "company" or the "corporation." "The State pays the bills," said a lawyer to me, after two of them had wrangled a long time about the stealing of several melons. Those were expensive melons to the State. Those two lawyers would have come to the point with less parleying had they paid the cost. The heads of government and of corporations do things that they as persons would not do. Lawyers defend villains as legal counsel whom they would scorn to defend as men. They would not, as men, become the hired servant of such creatures to help them escape just punishment. The work of some so-called criminal lawyers if accurately expressed would read, "The hired valet of villains to keep them out of prison, or off the scaffold." There is a mob spirit in the tradition of the profession. Am I severe? Go around the world where I have gone, and look into the faces of as many thousands of men in prison garb as I have seen, of every shade and color of skin, and you may be severe too. It is no favor to any criminal to encourage him to think he can hire a talented professional to become his servant, do his bidding, and free him from deserved punishment.

The most barbarous persecutions have been carried on in France, Spain and elsewhere in the name of the church. Thousands of their own best citizens have been murdered or banished at the order of Church dignitaries, who, as men, would have blushed with shame at such deeds. I believe many of them would have suffered for those same persons whose torture and murder they ordered or executed, if they had come to them as individuals. Members of city councils, of State Legislatures, and of Congress, at times vote away money like water, because the State pays the bills. If they took time to think "my neighbor pays for this, the tax-payers who elected me must pay these big expenses," many legislative bills would never be presented. The world needs to study the causes of its crimes and failures far more than it does. To first find the leak is the way to stop the water from entering the ship—the world has already been pumping too long to keep it afloat. The individual offender must be sought out and corrected. Generals, kings, and their minions who execute barbarous orders are men; they must be treated as such. Seek out the culprit, and deal with him. Cease to scold the times, the other party, or the world in general, and fix the blame where it belongs. Let the lawyer cease to lay down his individual manhood to hire out to the criminal for personal service. It would be more honorable to black his boots for money than his soul, and he does the latter when he lets a culprit out of prison to continue his crimes. A highly respected lawyer, speaking of the inmates of the State prison, said this to me: "These men are a hard lot, you can do nothing for them. I have gotten them out of prison on a writ of habeas corpus, on their promise to pay me, and they will go off and I never hear from them again." He knew those fellows had had every chance to prove their innocence before sentence was pronounced.

Men are helped into Congress by a hired agent saying what he knows is false to get his employer in favor with the people; he has laid down his individuality and become the attorney in the case. Women follow the fashion in the same spirit; they would not throw aside such good clothes and buy new in their own individual judgment. The ecclesiastic has all too long laid down his individuality and followed effete and bad tradition. Suppose every priest and clergyman were set free from tradition to act in his own personal capacity with this command: "Now, you stand on your own feet, you are responsible for all your own acts and words, God who knows the facts calls on you for frank, honest conduct." What would follow? Some would go on just the same, but many would throw up their hands in grateful freedom, and be the men they have wanted to be but could not. Do you say they have been dishonest? No, not dishonest, but held by the mob spirit of tradition. No one man can break those chains. The right ones in high authority might, if they would, but they are usually too old to change. They are fixed in a vise of lost individuality—frozen in the ice of an ecclesiastical glacial period that has been crowding down on the warmer regions and freezing out the true religious life. This is no time for discouragement, that ice is being thawed, but it has left much detritus that must be cleared away. Too many break away from God, the Bible and the church, and fancy themselves free. This is a fatal mistake; it is only from false tradition they should separate themselves.

INDEPENDENCE OF THE INDIVIDUAL.

The farmer seeks to get plants that will thrive on poor soil, and animals that give a good account of their feed and care. The same principle applies to man. The powers of the individual need to be so well developed that he may be independent of special favors, and will thrive on poor soil. Much of the aristocracy and many of the children of the rich have been a failure because they have been trained to dependence, and their own individuality has been neglected. Put them in fair competition with others and they fail. They were taught false notions of their own importance. In countries where labor is looked down upon as not the thing for a gentleman to do, and where only a laborer may appear to wait on himself, progress is slow through the loss of much good talent. Slaves do not often invent new machinery, drudgery absorbs their energies. It is free men, strong each in his own individuality and originality, who invent new ways and appliances of progress.

There are many people independent of any one as to enough income for their needs, who owe it to the world to stand for freedom and right. Some of these know if they spoke the truth about certain ones in power, of wealth, or office, they would no longer receive the greatly coveted invitations to receptions and social functions. Miserable bribes are these, the price of liberty. Too bad to sell one's birthright of freedom for such a mess of pottage. What would one give for a watchdog to guard his home if he could be bought off merely with a bone, or a "nice doggy, doggy?" There are far too many intelligent persons bought off by a bribe of flattering words, or an occasional bone from the tables of influential sinners against the State and the world. Many of these flatterers are not bad at heart, but they are so comfortable themselves they actually do not know they are taking more than their share. "You are choking the baby with your tobacco smoke, sir," said a mother apologetically to a smoker, and he was man enough to reply, "Well, baby, I beg your pardon, I did not think anything about it, my babies are used to smoke, and do not object to it." There are many such who, if made conscious of their wrong to others, would think it a privilege to know and stop it. It is no privilege to the individual to be allowed to go on wronging his fellow-men. If I am standing on your toes to raise me out of the mud and do not know it, it is due me to be told now, that I may step off and apologize. You will likely tell of it later after I am away.

Cowards in high places is the description that best fits many of those men who stand near despots. It is sad that men like the Duke of Alva and others did not have the courage to say to their sovereign, "Sire, that is a barbarous order, I can not execute it." The man who is making bad history for himself has a right to know it in time to change. The last word has not yet been spoken of many who have been excused "because of their times." They made those times. We owe it to our children to disavow and condemn the bad deeds of our forefathers. Near the time of his death, Philip II. of Spain felt remorse because he had been such a demon of cruelty for the church. There were those who knew it at the time, who were high enough in authority to have been entirely safe in telling him so, yet they urged him on to his infamous life and record.

The true greatness of the individual is the excess of his services above what he takes for those services. That was the type of Christ, Washington, Lincoln, and many others. One might be a great monster of selfishness like Napoleon, slaughtering men and dishonoring women, or he might be a great assassin like Abdul Hamid of Turkey. If any man is great he surely must be honest, and not do less than his part of service nor take more than his share of desirable things. When he is at this point he is merely on the level——if truly great, he must excel in these virtues. A rich man ought to be one who has produced far more than he consumes—not simply one who holds a large sum given him or gotten dishonestly. Regarding riches, men may be placed in three classes. One may die rich, that is, leave much that he truly added to the wealth of the world; another may die just even, that is, consume all he produced; and another may die in debt, that is, consume more than he produced.

INDIVIDUALITY OF THE CHILD.

No person has the right to so teach a child in the field of religion, science or business as to weaken his individuality in the sphere of his personal responsibility to God and the State. It is a recognized wrong to cheat a child in business, to sell him a worthless thing, or overcharge him in price. By what law of reason has the idea became current that any one may teach a child anything he chooses in religion? That is nearly the state of things at present in free countries. Christian, Roman, Mormon, Buddhist or Spiritualist, a popular sentiment claims the right to teach any and all of these and infidelity besides. Why let any one poison the mind of a child, any more than his body? Men claim that they may disagree in the field of religion, but they might lay the case before a competent authority on the question of the grosser forms at least. All of these religions have had a chance to vindicate themselves and show their fruits somewhere in the world. The principle of supervision and its benefits has been established in the Pure Food and Drug Law. If impure food for the body can be prohibited, then the time has come when the mind should have better protection also.

A sheep is useful to produce wool and mutton, and its characteristic is to follow the one in front of it. Man is not a sheep, he can produce neither wool nor mutton, and he must not simply follow the one who happens to be ahead of him. He is an intelligent individual, and as a child he must early be trained to think and act for himself. At the present time it is especially important to develop and to strengthen the individuality of the child for the following reasons: In these days of great speed in running autos, trains, ships, and machinery, there is often need of a quick and correct judgment and the mind must be trained for it. There are also many unworthy persons who are seeking preferment, or to secure some monopoly, or to get public sanction for bad practices. These people offer large inducements to talented young persons to do their bidding; they buy up newspapers, and endeavor to bribe or silence ministers, editors, and teachers who might condemn their conduct. In the same way they seek to secure the approval of respectable persons for their low amusements and extravagant personal habits. These conditions make it of vital importance to have our youth trained with a strong personality that can not be swayed or bribed into furthering the schemes of unworthy persons.

THE INDIVIDUAL AND SELF-MASTERY

A more vigorous and more wholesome public sentiment is greatly needed in the present crisis. We have already too long spoken of wrongs in general terms, and condemned the administration, the party, the church, or society. It is time to trace everything to the last person and fix the credit or the blame on him. It is individual men who give orders to build breweries and distilleries, who scheme to defeat justice, proclaim war and carry it on. We should seek out these men and treat them as enemies working against our country, our State, our community, your home and mine. When the world begins to more systematically search for the chief person responsible and to say, "Thou art the man," there will be a great check placed upon evil, and a great stimulus given to good men and good measures that work for the common welfare.

There are too many human sheep who produce neither wool nor mutton, and yet who, in the abuses and the ignorance of the past, follow the one that happens to be ahead of them. They are found in religion, in law, in business, in fashion, in amusement, and in society. We need strong individuals to lead the world, and also strong, sensible people to follow such leaders. No one is great unless he is great when he is alone. Livingstone alone in Africa was a great man; Napoleon alone in St. Helena was a spoiled, petulant child. This world can not succeed, nor can it continue as it is, with only a few great men and women; the persistent aim must be to make all after the same great pattern. The business world needs large coins and small coins, but it can not use bogus coins. The world has room for large men and small men, but it has no room for false men—for bogus men. We will not reproach the coin for its size, whether it be great or small, provided it be the genuine metal; neither will we reproach men or women for their size, provided they be made of noble metal, and provided they stand the test of true character and genuine worth.

CHAPTER IV

GOD AND MAN IN THE SELF-MASTERY SYSTEM

I⊤ is not necessary to prove the existence of God any more than it is to prove the existence of the sun. To the highest intelligence, God is as evident as the sun. The sun itself proves it has a Maker, a continuous plan, and a mind superior to it. God is spirit, man is a combined being—a spirit inhabiting and acting by means of a body. This is God's creation, and like His other work, is so complete as to make an attempt to separate the two, even in thought, very difficult. The blending and union of the two is so excellent that some deny the existence of the spirit. Some have denied the existence of the body, claiming all reality is spirit and that material is imaginary. God's work in blending spirit and body is illustrated by an artisan who mends a broken article so well as to entirely conceal the break.

The sun is to the material body what God is to the spirit. The sun in the past has stored away great riches in the soil, coal mines, peat beds, and forests. These, with the light and heat of the present, with the various forces of winds, rains, rivers and water power are the work of the sun for the body or physical needs of man. The body lives and grows by organizing the material the sun has produced. Blot out the sun, and very soon all life on the earth would cease. When one thinks of these facts it is not surprising that there are sun-worshipers. It would be very natural to thank the sun for his gifts. When one stops to think how much God has done for man, it is surprising that any can be found who are unwilling to thank God for His benefits. This must be because God has made man so well, that, like a good clock wound up, he can go on for a time entirely by himself. As

74

the body grows by appropriating material prepared by the sun and combined with some minerals from the earth, so the spirit grows by contact with God, the Great Spirit, and by learning of Him. As we are now in the material world, and only in the early twilight of our existence, we know but little of the spirit. Spirit is like force and electricity, which we can neither see nor understand but very imperfectly. We observe the manifestations of these, study their laws, obey them, and use them for our profit. It is but reasonable that we should do the same with the spirit. We need to study and obey the laws that govern spirit development and well-being, in order to guide ourselves in satisfactory progress.

Some facts can be expressed in fewest words in the form of question and answer.

Who is God?

God is the Creator of the universe, of this earth, and of all life everywhere.

Why did God create the universe?

He has an interest and pleasure in His own work and its excellence. He created this world for the dwelling-place of man.

Why did God create man?

He wanted the companionship and co-operation of beings somewhat like Himself, so He created man in His own image.

What qualities does God want in man?

Intelligence to know and ability and strength to act. Honesty and trustworthiness so that he will not do less than his part of the work, nor take more than his share of desirable things.

Freedom for each to think and act within his own sphere.

Why did not God create man honest, so he would do right by nature? Power can not create a man twenty-five years old, that is, with the experience and knowledge that are gained by experiment and the test of living with his fellow-men.

Has man power to create?

Man can not create, but he can so transform many things that it very closely resembles the creation of new objects. A pair, one man and one woman, can bring into the world new beings like themselves. These children are so undeveloped that the parents can shape their lives and habits, their language, their religion and their modes of thought very much as they wish.

Did God instruct man concerning his life and conduct?

In His Word God revealed the important things to prophets and teachers, and these were to instruct others; and thus man was especially instructed how to treat his fellowman and his Maker. The greatest teacher of all was God's only Son, who came to earth to be born like any person, except that God was His father and a virgin His mother. This son, Jesus, lived in an ordinary home, obeyed His parents, learned to work, and to read like other boys. He labored to support Himself and help the family like other boys and men. When He was about thirty years old, He began His special mission, which was to teach and show the people how to live and do their duty toward God, toward their fellow-men, and toward themselves.

Did Jesus teach men all they needed to know concerning their conduct toward each other?

He gave the great principles and rules sufficient for intelligent persons to begin with, and promised further help as it should be needed.

Is there any reliable record of these events?

The Bible is such a record. The Old Testament gives many facts regarding the history and duties of man up to the time of Christ. The New Testament furnishes a brief account of the life and teachings of Christ, and of the beginning of the Christian age and church.

Are there many questions about God and ourselves that can not be answered?

There are very many questions which can not yet be answered in all fields of man's activity. As a race, man is in the earlier stages of his development, and he is in part to work out his own salvation himself.

It is not important to discuss the question as to what God could do; it is better to limit ourselves to what He has done and what He is still doing. Evidently He worked alone for a time, then He called to His aid this whole universe. He prepared the earth for man, and then called man to aid in further developing the earth and its resources. Man's greatest work is to develop himself and the whole race of mankind, under the Divine direction and help.

GOD IS A FATHER.

Since God calls Himself Father and ourselves His children, we can learn many of our duties to Him by what we know of the duties of children to their parents. By knowing what the best parents' desire in their children, we can know much of what God desires in us.

Man wants his own child to be intelligent, strong and true. He would not keep him a babe if he could; he teaches him to walk and to talk as soon as possible. He wants him to stand on his own feet, and not be led by others, but rather to be a leader among his fellow-men. He wants him to become a fully developed, self-directing individual, an honor to his parents, to his country, and to God. Man is quite willing to have his own children more capable than his neighbor's children. God has no "neighbor's children," hence He is a better judge between man and man. A father can and will do better for a child that obeys him and tries to learn, than for one who is disobedient and refuses to perform the tasks given him. The same is true of God.

The father wants the companionship of his children; he wants a close friendship between them and himself. If they are out of sight, he wishes to hear from them. He wants them to come to him for help in genuine needs, but he does not want them to sit down and cry for trifles; he wants them to use and thus develop their own powers. God does the same with man. No father owning a large island, and having a number of children, would so divide that island inheritance as to give each a complete monopoly of some necessary product or privilege. To illustrate: The father would not give one son the monopoly of the fuel, another of the food, another of the water supply, another of the education, and another of the religious affairs and morals. The father would, for the sake of justice and to avoid strife, so far as possible make these necessities open and free to each and all of the children. We must then conclude that all monopolies are against God's will. Least of all would God give to any person or class of persons a monopoly of the way to reach Himself and heaven. God surely would leave the way to His house and home without gates or bars that might be in the control of one person against another. A servant who would not let the children see the father's will, and would interpret it to suit himself and for his own gain, would be regarded as an enemy to both. The conclusion then is this: Those priests and ecclesiastics who claim the right to stand between God and His children as confessors, who deny the people the use of God's will and testament, and who claim to have a monopoly of the way to heaven, are false teachers. The people who are thus deceived finally reject such a God and such priests. This is exactly what has occurred in Portugal, and to some extent in Italy, Spain, Mexico and other countries where the Bible has not been allowed in the hands of the people, and where the children have been required to make their confession through a priest. Portugal rejects God because He has not been made known to them as He really is. The people themselves say the priests have kept them in ignorance and poverty while they have claimed to teach them God's will; now they reject both God and the priests. It is not because they are Portuguese, for the people in that country who know God believe in Him. It is not the fault of true religion; it is the fault of a pernicious system of foreign domination, developed and carried on for many centuries as a monopoly in the interests of Vatican Rome. It is only fair to God and to Portugal that the Christians of the world should send the Bible and true teachers to that country to help the people to know God their Father as He really is.

Much of the teaching of the church has mystified God and made people afraid of Him. He has been represented as a terrible being inhabiting another realm, where man can not approach Him until he dies and is purified in some way by suffering. Certainly God is far above us in goodness, but He is still our Father, by His own Word. To illustrate: We are not to go to church in the morning and act as though God were there, and an hour later go on a frolic with the sinners and act as though God had stayed in the church and was unacquainted with our conduct. Honor Him in the sanctuary, but do not dishonor Him in the frolics of life. Some excuse themselves from obeying God because they do not know Him fully. The donkey is a good model in this respect. I have many times admired the conduct of that faithful animal as I have seen him in Mexico, in Spain, or in Palestine. He obeys the highest authority he knows and carries his burden patiently. He seems to make the best of his lot, and is fed and cared for by his master. If men were only as sensible with their Good Master all would go better.

Believing and Understanding.—Some say they will not believe what they can not understand. Let me talk to such personally. You do not understand electricity, yet you walk and work by its light with great profit to yourself. You do not understand God, yet if you will walk and work by His light it will also be greatly to your advantage. The power of electricity adds very much to comfort and speed in travel. So God will aid very much in the progress and growth of the soul and character. You respect electricity and obey its laws—you will not touch a live wire. You take the word of those who make a careful study of that subject and are competent to judge. Simply do the same with God and you will soon come to understand enough to lead you to seek earnestly to know more of Him. You say you are not asked to love electricity. No, but if you should learn that electricity is not simply a great force, but a person who knows you and loves you, would it not be a joy to think of such a one as your friend? I find it so with God, and millions have done the same. I have been in a foreign land in a strange room and it was dark. I obeyed a law of electricity, I turned a button, and it was light; that power had come to my aid. I was lonely. I obeyed a law of God, I called on Him, and there was divine Companionship, I was no longer lonely. Further, I did not need to seek companionship on the streets or in questionable places. Good company is not so easy to find as bad in a strange land. The bad seeks you in hope of gain, the good shuns you for fear of loss. Only one good, safe place do I know that is always open to the stranger—that is the house of God. I always feel a certain right in a church, even though it may be quite different from mine. The common people, at least, honor my Lord there, and that brings us nearer together. Wherever the missionary has preceded me and where the Bible is read I can find Christian companionship. I have done this in every land where my feet have wandered.

WORSHIPING GOD ACCORDING TO ONE'S CONSCIENCE.

There are those who claim the right to "worship God according to the dictates of their own conscience." This is a careless sentence that has escaped from loose thinking and has been allowed a measure of credit. With it is coupled a claim of the right to worship God or not, as one may choose, which is absurd. Let us look at this error. We are in respect to God what children in a good home are in respect to their father. He performs his part toward them, which leaves them no choice but to do their duty to him. It is their duty to obey him and give him credit for his benefits to them. Now, shall they perform those duties to their own satisfaction or to his? Plainly, to the father's satisfaction; his judgment must decide. The same is true touching our duty toward God. Worship is due, and it should be according to His will, not ours. Men require it so; the soldier, the sailor, the pupil in school, the apprentice in a shop, and the beginner everywhere fits himself to the authority under which he works. He does not claim the right to serve his employer according to the dictates of his own conscience; it is always the conscience of the superior that decides, otherwise the contract is broken. Thus it is God's conscience and will that must decide in what manner man must come to Him and worship.

Confession to God is as much as to say, I know more than I did; I am able to surpass my own yesterday, and I will acknowledge it to my Maker. It means progress, and He will be pleased to know it; never repenting and never confessing would mean no progress. In developing his own personality, man makes better advancement after he has recognized and sought the help of the Great Personality. God has given man such a distinct identity that one can hold out with God against all else. He can hold out against God, but at the loss of everything, perhaps even his own self and existence. Existence would be only a misfortune to him after that.

Adam's Sin.—I asked myself one day, Why did Adam sin? I listened intently, and this answer seemed to come to me—not from the dead past, but from the live future: "If the time spent on the criticism of our first parents had been given to the improvement of our grandchildren, the world would have been vastly better off long ago." I suggest this latter course be given a most vigorous trial. Some one in the past is to blame for hiding God in a cloud of mystery, and the glory of service in a fog of "drudgery;" service cheerfully performed is not drudgery.

SELF-MASTERY OF MEN AND NATIONS

Yes, and each can refuse, and most of them do. Luther, Wesley, and others were called, and they obeyed. God raises up men, and most of them do not like the work, and many take the talent He gave them for His special service in advancing the world, and use it for selfish gain or glory. So God and the world must wait until some one more faithful comes along. It is not like God to lay so large a burden on the shoulders of one man. Take the illustration of a father who has several children. He calls them all up in the morning to do the work of the household. Only one gets up; the rest are too indolent. Does the father lay the burden of supporting all the rest on this one? No; but if he will try to do it, the father will help him. It would disgrace the father to have even one child starve to death or die of laziness. He will help the one who will do more than his share, and thus save the family honor. God is dishonored by the life of every beggar, whether that beggar be rich or poor. Certainly God helped Luther and Wesley, and He will help you and me just as much if we work as hard and as unselfishly. These men stood at the turning-points of history, and had unusual chances to do important things. They did them, and now they have great honor when it is all over. Does any one covet the labors and hardships of men like Luther and Wesley? If so, there is a great, open field to be tilled, and God will help him win. One must have the spirit of those men and work for others, and not for himself alone. No farmer aims to raise one big ear of corn to a bushel of nubbins; he tries to raise all big ears. I think God prefers to raise all large men, not simply one to a generation. He therefore calls all men all the time to the field of great service.

Stand the Test.—The God whom I worship and the Christ whom I serve stand the test of my keenest searching and of my freest thinking, provided I remain within the boundaries of the truth. They can be proved by experience in storm and sunshine, in gains and losses of friends, in sickness and in health, in the first cabin of the steamer or even among Africans on the deck in the West Indies. I have not sought for God's presence in low dives, theaters, and midnight amusements. When a young man, I tested the most select companies and associations in the dance and theater realm; but, feeling out of place, and having a sense of the absence of God and Christ there, I left that crowd. I have never regretted the guidance and good training that warned me in time. I have gained a better companionship.

ARE TRIALS SENT FROM GOD?

Whether in former times God ever sent trials to test men, I do not know, but I can not believe He sends them now. The person himself, with the aid of his friends and neighbors, can furnish enough. I believe I have had my share of trials, but I can not trace any of them to God, neither have I any special charges against my fellows. I have tried to keep out of debt in other things, and likely, if my friends have been generous with me, I have paid it all back in regard to trials furnished. The best way out of any trouble is to avoid the path that leads into it. I do not think God has pushed me into trouble, but I know He has helped me out of many a difficulty.

The following is a reflection that came to me in Brussels, after wandering over the city and recalling its history and the lessons it teaches.

When man accepts God he comes to himself as one who had been in a long delirium of fever, while things had gone on unknown to him. It is somewhat like being born fully equipped, yet unacquainted with one's surroundings.

He asks: "What is this? Here is food ready prepared;

clothes that fit me; a house to live in; fields growing more food! I see life all about me. I have life, too. What is life? Who am I, and who provided all these wonderful things for me?"

God hears him asking all these questions, and comes to answer him. That is revelation, no matter whether it comes piecemeal from my parents and others in childhood, or whether it dawns on me in a few hours after the blank which a fever sometimes causes in the pages of life—I have known both. It is all revelation, and as I go along asking questions, God is the one at the end who answers the last question, and who thus reveals to me the whole circle; I had seen but small segments of it before. Then I ask, "Why did God do all this for me, and create me with a nature to enjoy it?" And the answer comes, "I wanted your companionship and your help in continuing and developing this world; come and get acquainted with Me." This I did, and now I know that none who become truly acquainted with God will ever wish to break that acquaintance. So I say: "I thank Thee, Lord. I want to know the One so great and yet so good as to make a place complete and excellent like this for me. What can I do for Thee? What remains yet to be done in this great system?" And a voice seems to reply: "The heavens move on in obedience to My plans, and the material things of the earth are being rapidly developed, but the race of mankind is far below its destined place. All the world can be raised to the level of the best at present. All peoples and nations can live as neighbors, and the *desire to be a better neighbor* can become a ruling passion in the heart of every full-grown man and woman. I have called you to aid Me in elevating the whole race. This is in your power, and this work will be your largest field of joy and satisfaction." These are the visions that came to me that July day in gay, sensuous Brussels.

GOD AND MAN IN SELF-MASTERY SYSTEM

God never put into man's physical being any elements or powers that his spiritual nature can not control and use for good. That would be unjust and unfair; that would not be "made in the image of God," as God has nothing in His nature that He can not control. There is no animal nor animal passion that can master man. By the same line of reasoning we can know there is no spirit nor group of spirits that can master the spirit of man. But man must call upon his partner, God, and make his preparation for strength. He is accustomed to get ready for great enterprises; he prepares for winter, or for war with his neighbor. Man is not a solitary being; he is made for partnership in all he undertakes. Man was made to live and work in pairs. Two are necessary for many kinds of work; two can dig a deep well—one works at the bottom, and one at the top to bring up the dirt with a windlass. Two can build a high wall or a house. Two people in a foreign land can defy the world for companionship, though they require the help of others for comfort and travel. We can not live alone, and we can not live in defiance of others. One can not be a successful sheep-grower if his neighbor raises wolves to roam at large. The same with children. If people with wolf-habits live near us, our children will not have a fair chance. Those who gain their substance by crime, by liquor, by unfair means, can delay the progress of the world. It is a great marvel that God endures such people who live by destroying others.

The whole world can be divided into two parts: one works, and pays its way; the other lives by plunder, preying on the better part. At times the husband and wife occupy these two different sides, and then there is woe to the better one and to the children.

There is great need that those whose hearts revel in luxuries should realize their partnership with those who

85

endure hardship in preparing those luxuries. Do you who ride in automobiles help to send missions to the toilers in the dark, dismal swamps where rubber for your tires is gathered at such cost in human sacrifice? Those who strut about in borrowed, no, stolen pinions of the songsters—do you not care that the birds suffer for your barbarous pride? You are one of a pair; the suffering birds are the other. Do not be a savage. Those are God's birds sent to cheer the whole land; let them live and sing. The progress of the world has lagged because the few in luxury cared so little for the rights of the multitude in need of many things. Ignorance is a poor excuse; each should seek to know what God wants done, and then do it with all his might. A good dog or horse will do as much as that for his master—his partner. There is one pair of supreme importance, of which God is one and each person is the other. This is a partnership of the most vital importance. When God and myself testify together, the fact in question is established; when we disagree, I must yield.

There are two witnesses available for every act of life; namely, one's self and God. The man who knows and trusts both of these does not need a boss to keep him at his task. He may work out of sight of his employer, but not out of sight of God. Oh, you business men who employ others, how much more it costs you to keep your men at work when they do not respect themselves nor God; when they will steal time and waste material if the eye of the overseer is turned away! It would be a vast economy to have all the business of the world done in personal partnership with God; then the employers would be fair with their men, and the men would all do honest work. It would be a great economic gain to have God as overseer for all partnerships of men; for corporations and patrons, for teachers and pupils, for merchants and customers, and especially for husbands and wives in the life-partnership of the home.

GOD AND MAN IN SELF-MASTERY SYSTEM

In closing this chapter let me suggest a hypothesis in proof of the reasonableness of God's method in managing this world.

If you could create a world, would you form all the heavenly bodies and the earth, set them moving like clockwork, and stop there? Would these satisfy you? No, they would not. Then suppose you could go on and add to this the whole range of plant and animal life, as we know the world to-day. Would you stop there? No; you would continue. You would want beings who could work with you more intelligently than the earthworm that loosens the soil, but knows nothing of it. Would you create a race of slaves to serve you by bringing you food and drink, and then to crouch at your feet as though you were an Oriental despot? No; so small a nature as that could never originate a world.

On the contrary, would you not create beings much like yourself; beings who could think, though they might think blunderingly for a time; beings with marvelous hands that could do much, though they might hurt themselves and others badly for a time? You could create them with the five senses, and give them bodies in which these could act; you could create them with great powers of intelligence; you could create them strong and capable—but you could not create them fifty years old. That is to say, you could not give them the slowly accumulated knowledge and experience that a wise man gathers in fifty years of living in this world among other strugglers—you could not create them honest. An earthworm is neither honest nor dishonest; it knows no code of morals. Intelligent men have to learn what is "mine and thine," and how to deal with the two, in the school of life. They must have the power of choice, they must be free, and they must learn to be honest and true to their Maker, to themselves, and to each other.

Let me tell you what kind of beings you would create if you were infinite in power and goodness. You would create beings suited for companionship with yourself: intelligent to know, capable to do, honest to be trusted, and free to act. You would desire beings who would like to come and be near you for what you are; who would like to know what you wanted done, and then go and do it joyfully with all their might. You and I like to have intelligent persons desire to be near us for what we are, not simply for what they can get from us with little trouble to themselves; we are not pleased with those who usually fail to appreciate us. You would create beings like ourselves, whom you could finally lead to a higher level of life and conduct; beings whom you might at last take into a liberal partnership with yourself, like the grown-up sons who choose the father's occupation and join forces with him in business; beings who would, after some faulty work, finally learn how to produce vigorous offspring, and then train them all into stalwart men and noble women; in short, if you were like God, you would do just the same as He has done.

A VISION OF THE FUTURE.

After wandering over the earth with the Son of God as my traveling companion, living among the busy people as He lived, and sharing their plain accommodations as He did, I raise my eyes and look. There is some obscuring fog near me in the valley, but yonder, on the coming horizon, I see no cloud of discouragement. The sky is clear; and it is God's sky—and mine. The sun shines, giving light and life; it is God's sun—and mine. I go to the summit of the mountain, over which I gazed in the face of the horizon, and look again. I behold a world-vision; it is God's world—and mine. He is winning it from darkness to light for Himself—and for me. He has invited me to come and help Him; I am going to do my best. I have a little money; it is God's money—and mine. I will not waste it on personal luxuries; I will deal fairly with my Great Partner. I have some strength and energy; these are God's—and mine. I will not use them in compelling my fellow-man to carry me; I will stand upon my own feet, and lend some help to God's younger children. I have some power of love; it is God's power—and mine. I will not bestow it on unworthy objects; I will learn to love what God loves. I have faith and hope in humanity; these also are God's—and mine. I am anxious to tell the world of the abundance and value of God's treasures, and how He invites all to come and enter into partnership with Him. I will go among the awakening youth in the schools and churches and enlist their interest and help in acquainting humanity with this knowledge and invitation. Will you not come too? and together we will sow the seeds of truth in the fertile soil of the human heart wherever man is found, and the coming harvest will be God's—and ours. In His Word you will find an urgent call to engage in this service. The unspoken prayers of millions of little beings, who have not yet learned to pronounce the words of petition, entreat you to come and help them secure their birthright. They have pressing needs, and so much good is possible now before evil enslaves them. Come and help, and some day they will delight to arise and call you blessed. "Inasmuch as ye have done it unto one of the least of these My brethren, ye have done it unto Me."

CHAPTER V

THE GREAT COMPANION AND SELF-MASTERY

THE principle of companionship is inherent in everything. It is the great principle of existence that holds things together. Particles of matter attract each other. Plants and animals reproduce their kind, live in herds and flocks, and obey the law of companionship. God wanted the companionship of beings somewhat like Himself, and created man in His own image. He created man with a companion and life-mate. Man alone can do very little, and would soon cease to be; he must have companionship. The question is finally reduced to this, Who or what shall be his companion? Shall his companionship be good or bad? will it help or hinder his progress?

It is often asked why the devil leads man astray. Bad people lead others astray because they want companionship; the devil may have the same reason. Certain it is that human beings will accept bad companions rather than none. Any institution that can furnish attractive companionship is sure to get some following.

God has provided one companion great enough and complete enough for every human being. His Son, Jesus of Nazareth, meets the requirement of every age or condition in which man need be found. This same Christ is our Model, Teacher, and Example in all acts or thoughts of life. Jesus was tempted in all points like as we are. All He taught was simple and natural to a right life, and practical in the application of its spirit to the every-day affairs of the world. His power and knowledge are complete. He was a perfect self-master even to the extent of life and death. He could excel every man, but He would not allow Himself to do any wrong to Himself or any one.

The great difficulty in taking Him as our hero and example is because we have been following the wrong system. We have followed the system which makes that person a hero who can master others and subdue them, whereas the Divine Hero masters Himself, and teaches others to do the same. He is not in another realm, as the heathen represent their gods to be. He was on this earth for a time as an actual man, and now is here a spiritual man, to help and guide the development of every individual in body and spirit. Either His life was a daily model for us, or it was a mockery. Had He said, "Follow Me," and then had advanced Himself by wronging others, or by grasping after wealth and power; or had He even lived in the luxury of many good people of the present day, it would have been a mockery. It would have been asking an impossible thing of common humanity. The multitudes of the world could not follow such a leader. Even in food, clothing, and personal luxuries the daily habits of the Christ had to be such that the multitudes of common humanity could follow His example. The keeping of His commandments implied following the spirit of His daily life, and included nothing that is impossible for the average people of to-day. He performed miracles to prove His divine power and authority to guide and save men. He said, "Greater things than these shall ye do," not in just the same way, but that the same desired ends would be reached. We are to follow His spirit in our eating, clothing, and all other acts. Not the same style of coat, nor of shoes, nor of food; but plain and wholesome these should be, suited to health and convenience, and not for display, as is too often done at the present time. If we were to follow His example in the one item of simple food, never over-eat, nor drink harmful beverages, it would defer many a funeral for years. It is a greater thing to keep a man well than to let him get sick and then heal him by a word of command. It is a greater thing to keep a man alive and well until he is old, and then have him die at the completion of his work, than to have him so careless as to die several times, and be raised to life by a miracle.

THE MIRACLES OF CHRIST.

A great deal has been written about the probability of miracles, and I used to be somewhat confused by these discussions. Now, after maturer study and experience, this is my position. The miracles of Christ are to be expected. They follow as a matter of course from the fact of His divinity and humanity. It is not the presence of miracles that needs explaining; their absence would have to be explained, and could not be. What is the great principle in a miracle? It is simply this: doing something that man could not possibly do in that time or manner. Man could feed five thousand people in the desert, if given time. Man can not raise the dead, but his business is to live according to God's laws, and he will then have no occasion to raise the dead. Christ performed no miraculous deeds just to make the people wonder. He as much as said His miracles were temporary expedients, and never to take the place of the regular course of events, guided as man would be able to guide them.

There is not one act in the life and teaching of Christ, required in the Christian life, that does not have some parallel in every-day life. Let us compare two events. Here was a multitude of people on the mountain-side, far from a sufficient supply of food. "How shall they be fed?" is the question asked. It was utterly impossible for them to feed themselves then and there. Christ fed them, and it was by a miracle. Here lies a new-born babe. He has life, and plenty of it; but that is all. He is hungry, like the multitude, and utterly unable to feed himself here and now. His mother feeds him, and it is a miracle to him. It was as impossible for him to get his own food in a few moments without help, as it was for the multitude. Every child that has the good fortune to be born in a Christian home has God and Christ fully represented in his own parents until he is able to do something for himself. He lives on miraculous acts every day until he is somewhat mature. He will never have any doubts about the facts of miracles if his parents do their duty in his instruction.

Why load such a natural event as the principle of miracles with a cumbrous definition, and then reject it? The theologians have done this in many instances. They have wrapped a cherry in a blanket, and then asked us to swallow it. The simple truth of God is the cherry, and their definition is the blanket. There may be a little stone in the cherry, but it need not be eaten. It has its place and purpose, and we have sufficient intelligence to take note of that purpose. So of many cherry-pits in various parts of the Bible. I hope to remove the blanket for the children of the future, that they may enjoy God's cherries of plain and simple but attractive truths.

Christ performed very many miracles, according to the gospel record; some to prove His authority and His power, but far more because "He had compassion on the multitude." I have often thought, as I have wandered through foreign cities and seen so much want and misery, "If I had the power that Christ had, I would perform more miracles than He did." Why would I perform more? Because I have a good deal of compassion, but not the wisdom, nor the judgment of the Master. Such bunglers as we are could not be trusted with so great power. The misery I saw in my extended travels can be nearly all traced to the misuse of power on the part of a few at the top in wealth and authority. As I can not relieve any of the suffering of the world by a miracle in the ordinary sense, I proceed to do it in what Christ evidently meant we should understand is a better way. This is to think of every man as my brother, and of his children as my near relatives; and then work, be economical, waste nothing, and leave them as large an inheritance as possible. The best legacy for them all is an inheritance of right understanding of the world, and of God's way of raising them to a high degree of excellence of life and character.

A JOURNEY TO EMMAUS.

Fully sixty thousand miles have I traveled over this earth with the conscious thought that Christ was my personal Great Companion. It has been a journey to Emmaus sixty thousand miles in length. Therefore none need wonder that I hold some gospel truths as securely as I hold the fact of the sun in the sky. The sun in the sky is out of my sight more than half of the time. Not so that Great Companionship.

I travel most of the time by miraculous means which I could not possibly supply without help. It takes a great deal of help by a host of people whom I never see. Many of them work by night, in the rain, down in the mine, at the mouth of the furnace, and in places that would be very unwelcome to me. Yet they toil on, and I am made comfortable and sped on my way by their help. All this is in the nature of miracles to me. Could I fail to be grateful to this multitude of faithful helpers the world over? Not when traveling with the Great Companion. There is then an atmosphere of luminosity about one that makes many things visible that would otherwise be hidden. I once saw, with the help of science, the shadow of the bones of my own hand in the X-ray apparatus. A Great Companionship is an X-ray to me, so that I see in the American, the Englishman, the German, the Italian, the Spaniard, the Mexican, the Asiatic, and the African the birthmarks of brotherhood. I see the man through the outer covering of race or nation.

COMPANIONSHIP AND CO-OPERATION.

There are two fundamental principles, which together can redeem and develop this world to its full capacity. The first is companionship. Almost every act of life can be reduced to two persons, or to halves, that must go together to make something complete. Two men are needed to do most kinds of work: a male and a female are necessary to reproduce their kind. Then there are the employer and the employee, the producer and consumer, buyer and seller, owner and tenant, and many other combinations. One alone can do very little; but united with a suitable companion, everything possible can be accomplished.

The other great principle is co-operation. Classify the whole race first into pairs of companions, and then let them all co-operate; let each do his part, and try to work in harmony with his other half, his complement, and the world's problems will be solved with surprising rapidity. First the man must co-operate with himself. His mind must co-operate with his body, his conduct with his highest interest, his income with his expenses, his strength with the load he has to carry, and his time of labor with his time of rest. These are a few instances of the application of the principle of co-operation in the individual person. Now apply these same cases to a company, community, or to any organized group of persons, and similar results will be noted. The following fatal mistake has been the enemy of progress. Instead of working together for a common end, and with the avowed purpose of not only getting full justice, but also of securing full justice to the other side of the transaction, each has tried to control it for his own gain. Each has tried to get all he could out of it. This is a war-principle and a destructive method, because it results in great waste. The waste comes from the fact of each being careless of the loss that appears to fall on the other party. The one who has some article or labor to sell has at times said to himself, "The sooner that purchaser is in need again, the sooner I can sell him another coat, or the sooner I can get another job of work." This has resulted in poor wares and poor work. There was a loss which in the end must be borne by both parties. The remedy for such loss is co-operation. Each must act not only for his own interest, but for the interest of the other party to the transaction. The theory of both these principles will doubtless be conceded by most persons who give the subject a little study. How to apply it is the great question. I believe there is but one path that leads to that City of Refuge. It is this: Both companionship and co-operation must begin at the very foundation of everything. They must commence with God, the Creator and Maker of all things. Each must combine with Him as companion, and co-operate with Him in every act and purpose. Further, each must combine with Christ the Savior of men in the closest possible union. The boy who goes into partnership with his father in a well-established business is in the way of great gain, because the father's purpose is to develop the boy's talent and the business, and finally pass it into his possession. That is God's position exactly, and the one who places himself in this relation of companionship and co-operation with his Maker and Redeemer will find the transaction to his profit in all things and to his loss in nothing.

One familiar instance will illustrate this principle. I must have a watch for my use in traveling. I am dependent first on the maker. I must co-operate with him by buying the watch and paying for it. I must also co-operate with him in caring for it; that is to say, I must follow his instructions in its use and preservation; careless handling would soon ruin the watch. In the second place, I must enter the relation of companionship and co-operation with a redeemer of the watch—one who can redeem it from the bondage of dirt in the wheels, or of a broken spring. I am like the watch; I had to have a Maker, and that Maker is God. I get out of repair even more quickly than a watch. I wind my watch once in twenty-four hours, and should have it cleaned once a year. I require some help oftener than once in twenty-four hours, and I need a general overhauling oftener than once a year. Then, like the watch, I must first have a Maker, and also I must have a Mender or Redeemer, to redeem me from the bondage of a broken commandment or a broken law of my construction.

For me to associate myself with these two, my Maker and my Redeemer, and fully co-operate with them, is for my gain in everything and my loss in nothing. As a boy I first was a companion with my father, and then co-operated with him in the work on the farm. It was to my profit in every way. Some of the neighbors' boys did not do this with their fathers. They left the work and went fishing, or to town, stayed out late, went into fast company, and had a good time, as they claimed. I was not allowed to leave the work for fishing or for doubtful fun. Later they had a hard time of it, when I had the freedom and opportunities purchased by companionship and co-operation with my father. Precisely the same is true, on a much larger scale, in reference to my companionship and co-operation with God and Christ. When all enter into this companionship, and all co-operate with their Maker and their Redeemer, then they will be companionable with each other, and will co-operate with each other. Things which are equal to the same thing are equal to each other. Persons who are true to God are true to each other.

THE REQUIREMENTS OF THIS GREAT COMPANIONSHIP.

Every item of this requirement is so natural and reasonable, and has so many parallels in our daily life, that I could explain it to an average class of children ten years old so they would grasp the ideas of the principles involved. It can be made so plain to them that, just as they begin the study of arithmetic and are led on to the highest mathematics, they can start on the certain road to a right life, and be led on to an excellent manhood and womanhood. Some would go faster and farther than others, but all would be on the right road, and all would get enough knowledge for their own needs. Every life would be a successful one in some field. Each would be made a self-master, to the extent of not doing less than his part, nor taking more than his share.

When one is to become a follower of Christ, to take Him as a companion, the first act is repentance and confession. One must be sorry for his wrongdoings and say so. Repentance is being sorry one has taken the wrong road through a forest, and admitting the mistake to the extent of changing to the right road. Confession means to acknowledge the fact fully to one's self and to God.

CONVERSION IS ALSO REQUIRED.

"Ye must be born again." Here is an old stove, broken, and of no use to its owner. This stove must be born again. The foundryman takes it, melts it again in the furnace, and pours the molten iron into the mold. He sets the parts together, each again reconciled to its new self, and there is the new stove. That stove has been converted. Do that with any sinner, and you have the new birth. Your sinner, broken and of no use to his owner, has been born again; he has been converted, he has become as a little child. He has become easily led to do right, and is willing to be taught his duty to God and humanity. It was a great gain for the old stove, as a stove, to be born again. Before, it was thrown out on the rubbish-heap. Now it has a place of service and honor. It is the same with the sinner. Before, he was a disgrace to himself and his friends; now he is an honor to both.

Sacrifice and self-denial are commanded in the religion of Christ. So they are in any life. Who denies himself more, in the end, than the one who becomes a drunkard, a thief, or other criminal, and an inmate of a prison? The whole difference is this. He denies himself good things in the beginning, and has a lot of bad things in the end. The follower of the Great Companion denies himself bad things in the beginning, and has good things afterward. Now, which has the better bargain? Which way are you advising and teaching the children, and which way does your example lead those who are watching you?

Here is a parallel. The soldier for centuries has given his liberty, his strength, his body to be mutilated, and his very life for others. Christ gave His back to the scourger, His side to the cruel spear, His hands and feet to the nails, and His life for others. What is the difference? It is this: The soldier gives all at the command of a superior authority, to keep a few persons in power over the many. He gives his life that the few may live in luxury, at the expense and labors of the many. Christ gave His life and all He had to make each one master of himself, honest and true to all, free in this life and in eternity. By the old method of sin every one lost much, many lost all. The despot lost in the end, even where he was supposed to gain at the time. By co-operation and companionship with Christ no one loses; all gain. Every one becomes a conqueror, riding in his own proud chariot. No victims are chained to his wheels; there are no weeping widows or orphans. His enemies were all within himself, and he has been helped to cast them out.

BAPTISM.

Christ Himself sanctioned the sacrament of baptism. The great significance of this act is that it is a form of initiation into the company of Christ's followers. Water is used as a symbol of purity. The real meaning of this rite is, that one becomes obedient to Christ and accepts the terms and conditions of membership in His church. It is a simple, impressive ceremony, required in part for its effect on the person baptized, and also on the church which he thus joins. Mutual vows of brotherly bearing toward each other are taken by both the new member and the old ones. There is no secret mystery or charm about it; it affects the spirit, not the body. It has parallels in the initiations into various societies which are almost universally required. The marriage ceremony is also similar. It is a public recognition of vows taken and binding on the two persons and the community. The married couple, as such, have rights that the community is bound to recognize. Neither the man nor the woman is now a subject for courtship by another person.

THE LORD'S SUPPER.

This sacrament was instituted by Christ Himself. In this service the fruit of the vine, unfermented and fresh, is to be used, because Christ gave His own fresh life-blood in sacrifice. Hence stale, spoiled grape-juice, commonly called wine, is out of place. The alcoholic product might represent the blood of a corpse, but not the blood Christ offered. Bread is eaten as representing the body of Christ, given, like the blood, for the redemption of the world. It is futile to claim any charm or talismanic power as existing in these consecrated elements. If one were to take them, not knowing they had been consecrated, or not believing in their sacredness, there could result no physical effect whatever. If it produced any effect for good or evil, it would be through the mind and the intent of the one partaking of them. If he meant to show contempt for what other people considered sacred, his act would have to be judged from that standpoint solely.

What is the meaning and application of Christ's words, "This is My body, and this is My blood, shed for you?" Plainly, that particular material was not His body nor His blood; it was such by representation, by symbol only. It was real, however, in that He did actually give His body and blood in sacrifice for others. It meant this for Him, "Before I will prove untrue to My mission, My teaching, and the cause for which I came into the world, I will give up My life; I will be faithful unto death." Now for us,

His followers, it means the same. I partake of the consecrated elements in memory of His death as He directed. I drink the fruit of the vine, and eat the bread, and imply in my vow, "I drink the blood of Christ in symbol, but it is my own that I offer in reality. Rather than prove untrue to my Master, I will give up my life as He did." Unless my vow is strong enough to include my faithfulness unto death, it is of little worth. So those words of His are literal in their meaning. Not the blood of Christ is actually offered in this sacrament, but the blood of His followers, each offering it for himself.

Those in power have been offering the blood of others in sacrifice all too long. Where is there any real sacrifice in that? A few years ago a desperate criminal was making his escape from prison. As he reached the gate he was seen by the guards, who immediately leveled their guns at him. Just then the wife of the warden was passing. The convict seized her and held her between himself and the guns as a shield, and the guards did not shoot. That was offering the blood of some one else in sacrifice. The same has been done, to the sorrow of the world, from the beginning until now.

The soldier, the policeman, the watchman, and all who stand between other persons and danger are expected to offer their own blood in sacrifice rather than to run away and desert the persons or the property they are delegated to protect. Is there any connection or relation between these acts and the sacrifice of Christ? There is a very close relation and connection. His example would make every individual true to the extent of giving up his life rather than his integrity to God and man. It would make war and all crimes impossible, for if a despot were to give a cruel order, it would be harmless, as no one would issue it or carry it out. There would be no reason for stealing, as the needy person could borrow or have something given to him until he could earn it. If earning it were impossible, there would be enough who would gladly share with him so much as was needed.

The failure of the church has been that so many would go to the sanctuary in all solemnity on Sunday morning and take the sacrament as representing the blood of another, and that only. After service they go to a sumptuous dinner. Then they go off on some frolic or excursion, still sacrificing the blood of some one else by compelling the trainmen and many others to give up their rights to the Sabbath day with their families and at church. The sham of such a communion sacrifice will finally be rejected. Already the world has detected this sham, and many are treating it with deserved contempt. The toiler is weary of the proud worshiper who devoutly bows his head at the name of Christ, but makes a mockery of His life and example. The conquest of the world for Christ would have been brief if all His followers from the first had imitated their Master's example in each offering his own blood and giving up his life rather than be untrue. A shame it is that so soon a few selfish leaders sought to gain the mastery over their brethren, rather than to sacrifice for them.

THE PROMISE OF CHRIST TO REDEEM THE WORLD.

There are those who reproach the name of Christ because so much time has elapsed since His coming, and so little has been accomplished. Can any explanation of this delay be given? I fully believe the delay is due to the following reasons:

Christ never promised to redeem the world by religion solely. That agency is most powerful, but not sufficient. Everything that contributes to man's well-being belongs to Christ and owes its service to the furtherance of man's redemption. Religion has done much, but education, business, and science have failed to do their part. At times they have stood squarely in the way of progress, and thus defied and thwarted the work of religion. If, instead of doing this, they had helped the true representatives of religion to rid her of shams and abuses, the progress of the world would have been greatly helped instead of being hindered.

The best service of education, religion, business, and science, together with the energy and enthusiasm of their leaders, ought to unite in seeking to redeem the race from all its sins and disabilities. Christ says, "Man shall not live by bread alone, but by every word that proceedeth out of the mouth of God." That includes the physical and the spiritual life. Christ came to redeem man from all ailments of body and soul. He therefore deserves the aid of every possible agency in so great a task. For the slow progress of universal righteousness, Religion should reproach itself, Education should reproach itself, Science should reproach itself, Business should reproach itself. Those who have taken no part in labors for the general good should reproach themselves. This would leave no one of those most concerned in these different lines much time to reproach the rest.

All agencies for good should be fully engaged in the closest companionship and co-operation in this work. As the individual man employs his hands, his feet, his eyes, and his intelligence for his own good, so must the individual race of men employ all its powers for its own elevation. God did not make any man's hands to be at war with his head, neither did He make any man's business or his pleasures to be at war with his religion. No man can have one foot traveling toward heaven and the other in the direction of perdition. Then he can not have his religion moving in one direction and his business or his science in another.

Everything Christ did and everything He directed His followers to do will endure the severest scrutiny. His work is genuine, and all of practical use. Everything can stand in the strongest light and be examined for defects and weaknesses. There are no shams, no frauds, and no empty forms. If any are found, strike them off; they do not belong there. I can assert the genuineness of a gold dollar, and stand before the whole business and scientific world and let them examine my claim. Will it rest on my word? Not all; it will rest on the reality of the gold. They will simply convince themselves of its genuineness. I can stand before the whole business and scientific world on the assertion that Christ is true, and just what He said He was. They may test all claims as severely as they test the gold dollar. The perfect divinity and the perfect humanity of Jesus the Christ will remain as unscathed and as surely genuine as the gold coin.

The actual facts concerning Christ are an interpretation of Him that every honest person can accept with profit to himself. By honest is meant one who is willing to do his whole part and not take more than his share. If any one is aiming to ride on the shoulders of his neighbor, does not intend to do his own part, and is grasping for more than belongs to him, he will not be satisfied with Christ. He will find the teachings of Jesus are a hindrance to him, though he will not be likely to admit the real cause of his opposition, even to himself.

Jesus the Christ has been grossly misunderstood even by many of His followers. All admit that He is good; but far too often He is represented as having an impractical, other-world goodness that is unfitted for this earth, and His system is regarded as having weaknesses and frailties that must be allowed special privileges and exemptions from close scrutiny. The actual facts are the opposite of this. Christ and His system will endure the severest tests known. He is the perfection of manly courage, business sagacity, scientific genuineness, and a masterful fitness for leadership in all possible beneficial movements. He is the exponent of true religion, true education, true business, and true science; and by true I here mean that which by its proper

use and genuine purpose works a benefit to all persons concerned with it, and which causes injury to none of these.

NON-RESISTANCE.

I have been asked to explain this doctrine as applied
to Christ. There is no such thing as non-resistance in His
system; it is vigorous with resistance; it is solely a question
as to where the resistance shall be applied. Shall I resist
the man who wrongs me, or shall I resist my temptation
to flog him? Christ resisted all temptation to do wrong. He
resisted the devil. He condemned the hypocrisy of the
rulers, He drove the dishonest traders out of the temple, and
He rebuked the rashness of His own disciples. He did not
resist personal wrong to Himself with physical force, but
He surely would not have stood calmly by and allowed some
brute of a man to torture a child, nor are we expected to
do so either. His teaching leads one to follow the course
of wisdom and good common sense in such matters.

Christ was putting out an utterly false system which
grasped everything for one's self and paid no regard to
the rights of others. He was putting in its place the true
system which gives little heed for one's own personal rights,
but would go to death rather than wrong and defraud
others. There was such an immeasurable distance between
the two systems that Christ, as the exponent of the new
order, seemed weak and impractical. The leaders of the
old system were so thoroughly fixed and steeled in its
iniquity that they were eager to murder the one who ex-
posed their wickedness and proved them to be false.

In seeking His own personal rights, Christ was meek—
He was a lamb; in defending and furthering the rights of
others He was bold—He was a lion. His methods were
those of honesty and justice, and not of violence; His
teaching would not allow two neighboring families to quarrel over a line-fence and a few feet of ground, nor would

it permit two nations to slaughter thousands of men in a dispute over some little province. He would call in the surveyor with his chain, for the two families, and institute such a degree of honesty and justice in the hearts of the two nations that it would matter little under which flag the disputed territory might be, and the question could be settled by peaceful arbitration or the ballot. There are far too many to-day who resist the man who tells them to be just to others and not defraud their neighbors, but they non-resist the ones who offer them empty forms for true religion, who tempt them to low-grade amusements, and who encourage them in personal luxury and extravagance.

In this brief statement I have given but a glimpse of the Christ, but I believe it is correct; I have brought only a cup of water, but it is from the inexhaustible fountain, and my aim is to send all others to the same source for their supplies. Any honest seeker may lay upon the complete system of Christ the measuring-rod of true religion, true education, true business, and true science, and he may also apply the tests of the most consummate common sense and practical reason, and he will find the Christ to exceed his expectation at every point; he will be filled with surprise and admiration at the magnitude and the eminent practicality of Jesus and His teaching to men.

CHAPTER VI

PRAYER AND SELF-MASTERY

PRAYER is a request to a being superior to myself in knowledge or power, for some benefit for myself or others that I can not procure unaided. Gratitude is the natural associate of prayer.

The principle of prayer is inherent in the nature not only of man, but also in the higher forms of animal life. Prayer is commonly restricted to petitions and thanks to God, but the identical principle of asking another for some help or something wanted is the commonest thing in life. This fact must be remembered, namely: that prayer is asking for what I can not do for myself. This is important, and must explain the apparently frequent denials of what we ask God to give. Often the thing asked for is to be gotten by ourselves through some means already in our power. All facts indicate that God desires my growth and development, and not to keep me a helpless infant; then He must put me on my mettle. Ofttimes He must throw me in the water and compel me to swim. We know well that many a man was made strong because he had to struggle, and thus learned his own powers. Take the best of us, and let us discover that by asking God we could get good bread, fruit, and vegetables, and it is very little hoeing and baking we would do. The race would degenerate rapidly. For our own good, God wants us to do all we possibly can for ourselves and others before asking His help. A good parent trains his child on this plan.

Prayer has been greatly misunderstood and, hence, abused. All sorts of incongruous things have been loaded upon it. To carry stone in a chariot or water in a sieve would not be more absurd than the use that is sometimes made of earnest prayer. The request is not granted. Some wonder and doubt, some weep and mourn, and some cease to ask God for anything. It will be noticed that they keep on asking their other friends for various things and all sorts of help. If I ever, so to speak, planted baked beans in my prayers, I have quit. I plant fresh raw beans, and then bake them myself or ask some one else to bake them. I believe in prayer as much as I believe in bread, water, or fire. It is as reasonable and scientific to pray as it is to eat food. My body grows by adding material; my mind grows by asking questions, and then building the answer into itself. My body assimilates the food—it does not simply paste it on; and my mind assimilates the answers— it does not simply pile them up as a dictionary holds words. Many a person is to-day a loaded train of passenger cars, with the engine fully equipped, the boiler filled with cold water, and the fire-box with good coal. All he lacks is prayer connection and Christ as the engineer to run that train up to the Dakota harvest-fields of human need and set that train-load of people to work for God and humanity, with himself as their leader and example.

SOME NEEDS AND CONDITIONS OF PRAYER.

I need to know and recognize my limitations in order to be persuaded to seek help in doing more than I could do alone.

I must know and believe in my possible development; that is, that God only gave me a start, and I am to take over this developing work into my own hands as rapidly as possible. I am not like the bee, born with knowledge enough to carry me through my course of life. I am created very incomplete. I am given powers and desires so great that I can not manage them alone. I must have help from my fellows; but that is not enough: help is needed that only God can give. To manage my powers and desires I need the example of other men, who excel me. I need the example, the help, and companionship of the Divine One, who lived as a man and proved what a self-mastered man can do. I need to see fellow-beings like myself struggling, losing, gaining, and finally victorious. I ask, "Pray, tell me how you did that?" They answer, "I asked the Lord, and He helped me." I see my fellow-men dependent on one another, helping each other where needed, checking each other in time of danger, spurring and pushing each other on as need may require, and thus progress is made.

Study the methods of a good, sensible parent in training his child, and you will learn much of the relation of man to God. Children ask a great many foolish questions, and are told to read, to notice, to think, and not ask so many questions. More and more we can help ourselves and others. As the child outgrows the need of its parent's help, and later becomes a parent, so can we outgrow some needs and become a supply to others. Older children care for younger ones, and thus relieve the parent of little things. There is crying need that we should do the same with our Heavenly Parent.

God is not trying to withhold any secrets from man that man can be trusted with. The banker does not give the new clerk the keys to the vaults the first day. This same clerk may become a trusted partner later.

That is what God is trying to make of you and me. We must, however, believe in Him and ask help in learning His methods, just as the new bank-helper must do.

Let me here give some of my own experiences in travel, as this is a better test than when one is at home, moving in an ordinary groove.

In Madrid, Spain, I hunted all day and did not find the room I wanted, but near night I found one that we accepted. As usual, we both prayed to God for direction and for guidance in finding a room. How do I explain the apparent failure? God would neither move any one else out nor build a house for us. I had no right to expect better quarters than the average busy people of Madrid have. Again, I wanted to know how the common people must live. I was there for that purpose. The trouble is that too many of the ruling classes in Spain have been selfish and have not cared how the common people live. Any day may be seen crowds of fine carriages and automobiles filling the wide boulevards in Madrid. They seem to be out to amuse themselves by the display of the evidence of wealth in their elegant clothes and costly trappings. I visited many churches, and was pained to see the lavish way in which money has been expended even there to gratify the love of display. The people are far too ignorant and too crowded in their houses. I know it better after being among them. We had only a small room, but the people were friendly and obliging, and we saw much of their daily lives. God answered my larger prayer to know my neighbors better. The common people of Spain are kind, considerate, and worthy, and I shall always count them among my friends and neighbors.

PRAYER IS SCIENTIFIC.

Prayer is scientific. My finite mind asks the great Infinite Mind to change me in some respect. This is entirely natural and reasonable. A wife asks the great heart of God to change the heart of her husband so he will love his family more and the grog-shop less. God sometimes does this. I should say, however, that that is a case for the men of the community to deal with; they ought to close all such places.

Again, did she know or did her parents know that the man drank before her marriage? are items of importance. We must not run heedlessly into danger, and then expect God to help us out.

It is claimed that prayer and its answers are mysterious. God does not try to make it so; as represented in the Bible it is very simple. As a child goes to its parent for help, so we go to God. Heathen priests try to involve prayer in great mystery, but that seems to be done to hold the people in their control. Prayer means that I recognize the fact that there is a higher and better being than I am; that there are fellow-beings more advanced than I am; that there is a better self possible for me than I now have, and that I care enough for this better self to admit my defects and ask aid in mending my ways.

If I wish to find a room in a strange city, and a boy can tell me, I ask him. If I wish to know the distance to the moon, and an astronomer can tell me, I ask him. I want to know the way to heaven, and God can tell me, and I ask Him. I hear that Christ will help me be a man and begin my heaven here, and I ask Him. I thank all these, return their favors if I can, or pass them on to others. If I wrong any of these I am glad to ask their pardon. Now, this is religion. It is scientific; it is sensible and reasonable. It keeps me at peace with God, with my neighbors, and with myself.

A carpenter builds me a house. I live in it, and after awhile it gets out of repair. Floors, windows, and other parts need attention. He comes and says, "Let me put your house in order." Shall I say, "No; this house is all right as it is?" I do not say that; I let him renew what is worn out, and he comes and puts everything in order. That house has now been converted; old things have become new. Christ tells me my heart or soul or self—call it what you will—is out of harmony and out of repair; I am not filling a man's place as I ought. He says, "Let Me set you right with yourself, your neighbors, and your Maker." I answer, "Yes, please do; I had grown careless; I am not satisfied with myself in this way." His help changes me; I become a new man; I am converted. That is a scientific act in both cases.

Repentance is a part of prayer. I took the wrong road;

I am sorry; I will go back and take the right one. I have taken the wrong hat—my neighbor's instead of my own; I will go and correct the mistake. In my haste and while excited I abused my brother man; I am sorry; I will go and tell him so, and ask forgiveness. I have not appreciated my Maker's gifts to me, and I have disobeyed His laws; I see my fault; I will tell Him so, and ask His forgiveness. Then I will ask Him so to strengthen my sense of wrongdoing that I shall not repeat these acts. These cases are all parallel; they are sensible, scientific, and only what any person would expect to do if well-bred, concerning his neighbor. Any man who will pay out a five-dollar gold-piece, thinking it is a new cent-piece, and then will correct his mistake and take it back, and be sorry he made the mistake, and vow not to do it again, has acknowledged the principle of repentance in all its bearings. The wrong act of paying out the gold-piece for the cent is very evident. If he takes five dollars from his neighbor wrongfully, he makes a bigger mistake than in the case of the cent-piece, and the result will be more serious. It will finally make him a thief and robber, and may put him in prison. Repentance is a very common principle and absolutely necessary in the ordinary affairs of life. Why draw the line between ourselves and God?

When I was leaving Foo Chow, China, I had to go to the boat before daylight in the morning. The way led through a winding course between high buildings, under arches, along narrow passages, where it would be impossible to find the right way without a guide. My friends provided me with one—a Chinaman, who spoke only a word or two of English. I must have help to find the way; I asked for it and got it; I paid the man and thanked him. He did not simply tell me, he went with me as companion and showed me the way. The child can not grow up with bad example and bad surroundings and be expected to find the way to a good life and heaven. He must have a guide and a companion whom he trusts and follows. Christ is that guide, companion, and friend for every child of earth. What good reason can any person give himself for refusing to come and get acquainted with Him and test His services and help? I can not pay the Divine Guide for His services as I do another man. I have so little, and He has so much. I can pay in this way, and this is what He wants; He wants my love and my loyalty to Him; He wants me to become trustworthy and tell others of Him. I can pass the favor along, and diminish human wrong and sin; and that I will do. Will you not help also? You would if there were a fire and your help were needed. Any neighbor would come to you in entire confidence, and you would go and help. Why will you not even more willingly give your help to save your neighbor's children from peril than his house from fire?

The office and use of prayer is also to bring the spirit into touch with its Creator and make it more like Him. It is to get more of His power and capacity, and with these to develop and master self and the circumstances about one. The child, by obedience to the instruction and example of his teacher, outgrows the need of an instructor. Shall we outgrow the need of so much help from God? Certainly. Christ said, "Greater works than these shall ye do." It is a greater thing to live above need of help than it is to have a permit from the poor commissioner to get groceries at the expense of the town. Better live without stealing than to have to repent for theft. After the prodigal returned, there was no reason for his going back to his old job with the swine.

DIVINE HEALING.

Many believe in prayer to God for healing from sickness. That is my firm belief, but this method is temporary. We call it divine healing, and such it is. The greatest instance of divine healing I have ever seen or heard of is the banishing of yellow fever from the Panama Canal zone. It will be claimed that was done by science. Certainly; but all the materials used and all the talent employed were from God. Miraculous healing was not used as a permanent remedy. Christ never performed any "stunts" to surprise the people; neither did He give to priests or others any such power, to astonish the crowd. His teaching goes to show that we are to use all His gifts to some account. We are not to step into the same mud-hole repeatedly, but to repair the road; that is, to stamp out disease. It is well established that the mind affects the health of the body. Now, a mind that has come into companionship with Christ and has become strong, can by that gain better resist disease. Jesus slept during the storm. So can you and I if we have sufficient mastery of ourselves. There is no teacher in this like the greatest of all teachers, Christ Himself, who went so far as to be master even of life and death. That is beyond us. We could not yet be trusted with that power; we might be tempted to start a show-business. Great sums of money are gathered by spectacular means in some parts of the world where I have been. Various miracles are said to be performed—with a cash attachment.

I keep my health in part by prayer. In answer to my prayer to God I receive strength to stop eating in time, and leave out a great many things not best to eat. That is far better and greater than healing by any means known. Under the example and guidance of Christ the spirit will discipline and train the body, and the two working together will be proof against ordinary disease. An armored vessel fears only the extraordinary enemy, such as torpedoes or mines; small shot do no harm to thirteen-inch armor-plate.

"Give us this day our daily bread" did not imply that it be cut and buttered. A brush-covered field and energy, seed and harvest, the threshing, the mill, the bakery—and it is done. Oh, what a joy to do things for one's self! I do like to be independent. I find it very hard to be patient in sickness—now twenty years since my last experience—because I prefer to wait on myself, and I like my freedom. Self-mastery gives me freedom from evils, and Christ helps me to self-mastery. It is both scientific and it pays; I recommend it strongly.

One can not commune with God and Christ in prayer without being stirred into a desire to grow like them. Let boys read about bandit heroes, and they are led into crimes like theirs. Let them read of true heroes, and they want to start out and follow these. Boys and girls can be easily led to take good models for heroes if they are properly taught. At present there are too many influences on the wrong side. Too many follow the low types heralded with wood cuts and big headlines in the papers of the day.

When a man begins to pray, he does not by that become a young bird with open mouth waiting to be fed. Rather he becomes a parent bird, using his wings to gather food for others, or material for a family nest.

Shall we ever outgrow the need of spiritual food by prayer? The body does not outgrow the need of material food while it lives, not until it dies. Hence we can infer that so long as the spirit lives it will need and will surely wish to keep in close touch with the Eternal Spirit.

Notes from my diary at Florence:

"I am sure God knows I am in no danger of becoming too strong and independent, like some rebellious province of a kingdom, if I am only honest and can be trusted; that is, so long as I do not less than my part, nor take more than my share. God could trust His own Son with all power in heaven and on earth. It will pay me to be honest, and thus gain all the liberty God can give. If I ask unselfishly, I am told to ask in faith. You have seen a child come timidly to ask the parent for something the child knew should not be granted. We do the same with God.

"It seems absurd that any man should not employ every known agency in the development of his spirit as readily as he uses new conveniences for his body. Prejudice and tradition should have no more weight in training and controlling a spirit than in the mode of travel across the country. A pope or a bishop should be as ready to change his methods in spiritual matters and church work as he is to change from riding a donkey to the railway or tram. The man who boasts that his religion has not changed in fifteen hundred years should live in other things in the manner of those early times. When one sees how the clericals in these countries adopt new ideas for bodily convenience, but refuse to grow spiritually, it is not surprising that they are losing the respect of intelligent people."

WE DO NOT OUTGROW PRAYER.

The young child has at first to ask for everything, later for less and less, and finally he provides for himself and others; but he never outgrows the need of gratitude for favors. My father has been dead over forty years. While it is long since he did anything for me, the value of his example and counsel grows on me. My feeling of gratitude to him for giving me a good chance from the beginning, increases from year to year. I can never outgrow these. This increasing gratitude is a part of my growth. I can not even outgrow the need of God's help in feeding myself. He supplies the raw material of soil, sunshine, and rain, though He does not plow and hoe my fields—I prefer to do that myself. My parents gave me the teaching and early light to see that life is happier in every way to him who helps himself. Later, as I knew God better, I saw that service to others is the law of God that makes Him great and wonderful. A god that did nothing for others would be a very small, useless thing—a human being likewise. If I can become more useful, I shall be greater. Thus I shall never outgrow the need or, more correctly expressed, the privilege of prayer. Even the suggestion of giving up prayer is absurd to me, though many seem to boast themselves as being above asking God for anything, as if they had lived past that point. I shall come to the place where I shall not need to ask for any more food or clothing from this world. I shall even give up the material of this body—lent to me so kindly for a time. It will then become common property for the first plant that sends out its rootlets to weave into some new mysterious life what had served me so well in mine. I expect to be then where I can say more directly: "Lord, I thank Thee for that one hundred and fifty pounds of earth, marvelously built into a human habitation for my more wonderful spirit for so many years. Thou didst keep me when a helpless infant, and didst bring me to maturity. Thou didst take me into Thy divine partnership in the care of my body and spirit. Thou didst help me gain the battle with my own selfishness, and didst open the great world-vision to my view."

It is not the province of prayer to entreat a pure being to take a vile beggar into his parlor; but prayer may well ask for a dish of water, that he may wash himself. If he will not do what he can for himself, he lacks the spirit that could expect help from God or that could fit him for divine company.

I arrived in Lisbon, Portugal, at two o'clock in the morning. I had not planned it that way, but found I must go on at night, as there was no other train. There were hotel agents enough for high-priced places, but I was traveling at moderate cost. I knew no Portuguese, but one agent, who spoke Spanish, offered me a room at a reasonable price, and I went with him. "It is just a little way," he said; but I found it quite a long way. The people had retired; but finally he got them up to open the door, and I saw my room. It was on a wee bit of a court, where the sun did not come, but the chickens did. They were not such bad neighbors, since they spoke the language I had heard them use in my far-away boyhood home. The next day I hunted for a better room, but not knowing the language, I could not make a thorough inquiry, and finding the prices too high, I remained where I was. The hotel people were plain and friendly, and they treated me honorably. I have only kindly memories of the Portuguese people as I met them in their country. It is the ruling classes that have been unfair in that land. But how about the answer to my prayer in finding a room? It is very simple. If such beds as I want are full, I am not to expect God to get some one out and let me have his place. He may help me get a place on the floor, as we did in my boyhood when we had company. He will help me be content with what is available. If I have been properly trained in self-mastery, I shall get along as well as the soldier, the sailor, and thousands of other worthy people. Prayer teaches one to be reasonable, unselfish, and sensible.

UNANSWERED PRAYER.

How about deformed children, persons in great distress and poverty—will God help them in answer to prayer? If He is to blame, or if that is the best way, I think He will. But the question is, Who is to blame? God will let a child put his finger on a hot stove twice if he wants to. The hot stove is doing its work and can not stop. The child will soon learn better; but if still too young, some one else must learn for him. God can not be expected to send an angel to choke off every well-fed person when he has eaten enough, and thus protect his health. Would you want to be the angel to do such work as that? How long since the first warnings were given against wine and gluttony? Yet men continue both, and their results follow. Many ask help from God and the doctors after the penalty begins. In cases of this kind the following is the element of prayer that is needed, "I repent of my sins and stop committing them, whether directly against God, my neighbor, or myself— soul or body." Not more faith, perhaps, but faith applied in a different way is what is needed—a faith that uses all available helps now, and asks God's aid for anything He can do further. He may indicate the next step, but may not pick me up and carry me.

Many little things go to confirm my belief and practice in prayer in every-day affairs. All through the thousands of miles of travel and study I have lived in a prayerful spirit. That means this: I never assume that I know all, and can learn nothing more on any topic. Just the opposite is true: I do not know it all, but I know enough to learn more. I know God and my fellow-men are ever willing to help me if I ask them in the right way, in friendly confidence, politeness, and faith. Thus I get help everywhere and all along the way.

Prayer is so simple, so natural, and so practical when properly understood and after the right habit has been established that it is much like the breathing of a healthy child, which goes on without thought unless some hindrance occurs like a cloud of dust or smoke. I ask so many small and great favors of God and man as I travel that prayer in action becomes very much like the lungs in action. Perhaps more like the digestive system, that labors whenever there is work to do, and is ever ready for service. I believe in prayer and use it as surely as I believe in shops, boats, and railways, and use them. All are necessary to me, and I do not need to grade them and say which is the most important; doubtless each becomes the most important at the time of its particular need. When I need what God only can give, I ask Him for it; when what only the railway agent can furnish, I go to him with my petition, and the same with the grocer and others. In each case it is my inexcusable duty to render whatever is due in return. To God it is thanks and service, making good use of His gifts; to the ticket agent it is cash and a courteous, brotherly bearing; and the grocer—the Golden Rule applies here—I must not require him to deliver some trifle that I can just as well carry home with me. My honest confession is this: The more common sense, knowledge, science, and business methods I use in my daily affairs, the less cause there is for troubling God or men for special favors. In all the ages I shall never become so capable as to outgrow the realm of please and thank you. I shall always have to ask God and my fellow-men for companionship, and for help to attain graces in which they are richer than I, and for these I certainly shall be glad to give credit. Who is the man who will not pray? He is the man who refuses to say please and thank you to God and his fellow-men. I would not want God and my neighbors to think me such a man as that. I am sure a feeling of insupportable loneliness would come over me if I believed they thought thus of me. That moment shall never come.

London, August 2d.—I spent an hour in prayer yesterday morning, seeking the best way to Boston, and as I was unable to reach that place without the aid of a steamship company, I went to their representative, asked politely and in faith for information and help. Faith and works are necessary. I must watch, and ask again and again. In religious matters we say, "watch and pray;" but I fail to see any difference, either in theory or practice, between religious matters and other things. Down on the Central American coast I watched for the steamer, then waited several days for the handling of cargo before the boat started on. The same happens in the Christian life. Was money needed for my passage? Certainly, or service; sometimes they let a poor fellow work his passage. Christ does the same. I do not see how either can use a shirk. The same rules apply in going to Boston as to heaven; it matters not whether that heaven be here and now or one hundred years hence. Surely my neighbors will never say I was too respectful to my Maker, and God will never say I was too polite to my neighbors. Both will more likely say he was too anxious to get his own rights.

In a certain part of England unusual rain was spoiling the hay, so it could not be cared for at all. Prayers were offered in the churches for dry weather to save the hay. This answer might well be sent, "Stop spoiling barley and other grain in making beer, porter, and whisky, and save them to feed the stock." Their common sense ought to tell them as much as that. Only by this principle am I able to travel wherever I wish. If it works well for a grown-up farmer boy, it ought to work for bishops and members of Parliament.

There was a serious strike of the London dockers, and a strike-leader addressed great crowds of men and had them repeat a prayer for the death of a certain government official whom they regarded as standing in their way. My suggestion and my practice is, "Pray for the death of the desire for drink, tobacco, and gambling, and save that money for food." These are genuine enemies of the men, and far too numerous, as I saw myself in studying the situation. There is a serious question as to that official being the enemy of those men. Better strike the enemy in an arm's length of you with his hand in your pocket, than to try to hit the one a mile away.

Here is a practical illustration of the field of prayer and its limitations. I asked a banker for money on my letter of credit. I asked in faith, and at first he was going to grant it. Then he noticed that the letter was limited to June 14th, and it was now August 17th. He asked instructions from the central bank, and they told me to come in person to them. I did so, praying that the technicality might be waived in my favor, as the letter provided for an extension of time on request of the owner. I was anxious, as there was no time to lose before the steamer should sail from Southampton. My prayer was not granted, but the banker said he would write to the issuing bank in Leipzig, Germany, and have a reply sent by cable. I feared there would not be time for that. Then said he, "I will send a telegram for reply at your expense." This I paid. I had done what I thought was my whole duty, but that was not enough. It was plainly written in the letter of credit that it expired one year from date. The banker paid one draft without noticing it, and I had forgotten the limitation. The banks kept their contract, but did not grant a special request from me. This illustrates prayer to God. We know the conditions of being heard. If we neglect to keep ourselves informed and in line with His laws, He can not be expected to encourage our carelessness by continued special acts and favors. "I did not know" could often be answered by "You might have known, for it was plainly written in the contract." On Monday I went to the bank, found the answer had arrived, and the time of the letter had been extended. I thanked God and the banker, drew my money, and hastened to the office and bought my steamer-tickets to Boston. Now note these facts: There is no line of demarkation to be drawn between the faithfulness of God and that of the banks. They are all part of His great system for man. All rights are sacred—my own and those of the banker, the mutual courtesy and confidence due to each, and the gratitude and brotherly love due to all.

The churches and others have made a bad blunder trying to divide life into sacred and secular. No such division will work. In business each has sacred rights, and God has a sacred right to man's integrity. Religion comes into business to require that man should be courteous, kind, obliging to a friend or stranger; but he must be honest with his employer, and not endanger the integrity of the bank to its other customers. Many a bank has failed by granting the importunate prayers of men who asked special favors of them. God can not run His Kingdom by rules so bad as to break a bank. The only fault is in not recognizing God and His gifts in all our affairs, and in not applying our knowledge to all life's business. How did I get what I wanted—my money, and tickets for the ship, and relief from worry while waiting? The agencies employed were these: Prayer to God and men through religion; business through the banks; and science and business combined in the telegraph and cable. Here we have all the great agencies man uses and must use so mingled together that they can not possibly be separated, and education teaches us how to apply them. The scientist and business men ought to be the most faithful in religion, because their mistakes can be most easily seen. A German adage says, "The doctor covers up his mistakes with dirt." The banker can not bury the blunder of paying a forged check so easily.

A complex prayer was once answered when I wrote for more money. The government, the mail clerks, and postoffice employees helped answer that prayer. All of them worked with God's material and the talents He gave to men. I received the money, and I thanked God and all the persons who helped me get it. I find this spirit of gratitude to all who have helped me, to be of untold value in my personal happiness. Gratitude is a comfortable feeling to me. Traveling so much puts me under obligation to a multitude of people the world over; so I have a comfortable feeling toward the whole world. Now, I learned this from my Great Companion through the agencies of a Christian home, the Church, and the Bible. I utterly fail to understand the man who does not find a pleasure in recognizing these helps and using them. Therein lies the whole essence of prayer.

When I went to Madison to engage a house to occupy while preparing this work for publication, I did not find what suited me. I prayed and studied over it, discussed it with my wife, and worried a little in the night. Finally I decided to call up the agent the next morning by telephone and take the best of several choices. Again the science and the business of the telephone helped me. Where did God come into this transaction? In both the business and the science employed, and in helping me to be content with what I could get and make the best use of it. Perhaps He knew some reason why this was the best place for me to do my work. I strongly incline to that belief after a good many years' dealing with God in all sorts of emergencies. You would trust an old friend after years of proof, would you not? I would, for I want my friends to trust me. The telephone ought to teach men to pray to God. Here they talk to persons whom they can not see. You say they hear an audible voice? A multitude of credible witnesses say their spirit hears a spirit-voice answer when they talk to God. I will stake more on some of my spiritual impressions than on my physical, for I have been deceived by both my ears and my eyes.

I do not make prayer too commonplace. My aim is to show that it is as common as asking favors of each other and as reasonable. The great activities of life can all be ranged under the departments of Education, Religion, Business, and Science. Prayer is a faithful messenger train that stops at all these stations, for the convenience and necessities of travelers. When the true province of prayer is once recognized and understood, I believe the last reasonable objection to it will vanish like night before the morning sun.

CHAPTER VII

THE NATION AND SELF-MASTERY

THE nation consists of the whole people working as an individual or unit for its own highest welfare.

The nation itself, as an individual among other nations, must be intelligent, capable, honest, and free.

The first aim of the nation should be to see that every child born within its borders becomes a self-master as early as possible; to see that each one is able to police himself, to support himself, and to pension himself.

The first duty of the nation is to safeguard all that goes into its make-up, and to care for the individual units which compose it.

These are:

The individual man and woman.

The individual family and home in which these two live and train their children—the future citizens.

Any organized group of persons within the State becomes a unit or individual, and as such is subject to all the requirements imposed upon the individual citizen. The churches, political parties, societies (secret or open), labor unions, or other organizations become units in the make-up of the nation. As the central intelligence of the man must supervise and control all that becomes a part of himself, so must the nation supervise and control all its own members and ingredients which enter into its make-up; only thus can it become free and self-mastered.

THE RIGHTS OF THE UNBORN.

For thousands of years the world has looked to its kings and rulers for improvement. These have had their say and their way, and they have failed. Now we must face

125

about and look in another direction. We must look to the child; he is king; his needs must be obeyed first.

It should be the determined aim of every generation to transmit to its successor all its virtues and none of its bad debts and vices. I do not see how one can commit a crime reaching further in its effects than to become the father of an illegitimate child, and then to desert its mother and leave his own child a burden to her or to grow up by chance. The young woman will have the double task of caring for the child alone and of bearing the shame of being mother but not wife. Yet there are so-called human beings who will joke about such a crime. There are too many others who will receive the father of a bastard into good company, and cast off the child's mother. Society, we ourselves, have a grave responsibility in cases of this nature. The nation needs to master itself to the extent of allowing such a man to become the father of no more children. Science knows how to do that, and if there be any sentiment of mercy, it is due to the innocent unborn. Such a man has forever forfeited the right of parenthood. If he was misled by others so far as to become a father, let him become the husband of the child's mother and make the best of it, and his child will then have some chance in the world. I can very well imagine a child who had been deserted by his father coming to his mother and saying, "Other boys have a father to support them; where is mine?" Then the awful revelation would have to be made that his father had betrayed his mother, left her in disgrace, and sneaked off, a contemptible coward. What made him so mean? How did he become so low and despicable? Who is to blame for such villains? These are questions for the nation to ask itself, and then follow that beast of a man backward to his den and see where he lives, learn who taught him bad morals, and who failed to teach him better ways.

The church, society, science, and business all have to share the blame. It is now time for each of these to shake itself free from the reproach of the past, and to do its duty in the future. Money is made out of prostitution; science helps cover up the crime, and one great branch of the church forbids its priests to marry, though it is often lenient with those of them who become fathers. Society keeps men and women in close bodily embrace at midnight hours, to dreamy music, after being surfeited with sumptuous food and drink. These same society people demand that the ministers in the churches shall keep silence on this shameful sin against God and against the home and parenthood. They have the audacity to bring pressure to bear upon the pulpit to have their vices condoned, and even commended. The influences and paths which lead to the crime of bringing illegitimate children into the world are many. Anything that leads to a low-grade life tends that way, especially whatever feeds the tiger nature of the animal in man. Such pleasures are bought at an awful price to many men and women, but the worst falls on the blameless and helpless children.

FLORENCE, ITALY, April 23d.

"The State must protect itself from bad citizens. This is done now in part by prisons and reformatories, which is a very defective, enormously expensive, and fatally wrong principle. No one tries to straighten a tree after it is a foot thick; the straightening is done when it is small. So must the State do with the character of its citizens. The State must protect its unborn children from a bad parentage. If the parents are so deficient in intelligence and principle as not to care, then the State must act. Any person has a right to curse the intelligence and power that allowed the unfit to bring him into this world crippled by disease or moral taint. The past has some excuse, but the future will have none. To-day it is known that certain ones are totally unfit for parentage. Drunkards, criminals, gamblers, beggars, and persons destitute of moral character are plainly unfit; they leave indelible taints upon their children. Let us deal with these first. We who possess the intelligence and power of control are under obligations to prepare the unborn to keep the commandment which requires children to honor their father and mother. By this principle only those who are worthy are fit for parentage, and no nation can prosper unless it has many parents worthy of honor. Every defect reflects dishonor somewhere. Men have been blaming God or nature or something outside of themselves. This is cowardly, since we know that God has given us great power of control over our own futures. The farmer controls the breeding, the feeding, and the general life of his stock for their good. We can do as much for posterity if we will."

DUTY OF THE NATION.

The great work of the nation is to safeguard the birth and early development of each individual citizen. The strength of the nation depends on the strength of all its individuals. The nation that was composed of a few great barons and a mass of serfs was neither great nor strong. The nation that is composed of a number of millionaire merchants and manufacturers, and a multitude of dependents and pensioners, is neither a great nor a strong nation. When each individual is strong and able to maintain his individual rights against the foes within himself, the nation need have no fear as to its ability to maintain itself against any foes either within or without its borders.

The weakness of the Central American governments has been the weakness of the individual citizen. The people have been taught to follow a leader, instead of being taught to follow their own good sense and judgment. When some aspirant for office, with little regard for the rights of others, goes out and makes great promises to the ignorant, poorly-fed populace, they follow him to battle and to death. The citizens who have been trained to police themselves will be much happier, more contented, and will relieve the nation of a great care and an enormous expense.

When people have earned and saved enough to pension themselves, this sum will furnish a vast capital, which young men may borrow at reasonable interest, and thus the world can go on improving itself indefinitely. The present rather rapidly-growing pension-system may do for a ferry to allow a hurrying caravan to cross the stream; but once on the other side of this emergency, the far better method will be for each to pension himself. Of two men, twenty-five years from now—the one a self-pensioner and the other having a pension from some company or the government—the one who has pensioned himself will hold his head a little higher and feel a larger measure of satisfaction with life in general. Those who are recognized as self-made men are rarely ashamed of the job. There is an element in every man's nature that likes to be free and independent of others. If the hope of independence through self-pensioning were held up before the children with proper instruction as to its benefits, and safe investments were assured them, what bushels of pennies and dimes would be treasured up for future use, instead of being worse than wasted for trifles that fix the habit of wasting!

People use money wisely or foolishly as they are taught. As in other things, some are more apt that others, but all can learn enough to care for themselves without a guardian. Bad instruction is given by dealers crowding their wares on to children and older ones. Slot-machines for selling sweets, and pop-corn stands on the corners are a nuisance by teaching children to spend money. If these were replaced by machines for selling savings-bank stamps, as is done in Germany, it would be a vast gain. Americans could well learn valuable lessons in matters of table economy from the Europeans when they first come to this country. They are strong and hearty, which proves a sufficiency of food; but they live far more simply. Unfortunately, after they have become prosperous, most of them learn the foolish ways of Americans and overload their tables. If we set only plain, wholesome food before our children, and teach them to study themselves and master their own tastes and appetites, we do better than leave them rich: we leave them strong and independent enough to take care of themselves.

Man is made to have most of his pleasures in the realm of the spirit, and not of the body. To me the consciousness of mastery over my own tastes and appetites is an almost constant pleasure, by the privilege it gives in the larger field of freedom from pain, and the liberty of buying what I prize much more highly. If everybody owned a home, and all the prisons were turned into factories; if poor-houses were not needed, and war a thing no longer feared, I could increase my luxuries without increasing my expenses; for without these terrible drains on the world, living would be so cheap that all might enjoy a plenty with moderate labor. Is not such a mastering aim worth more than big dinners, luxurious railway and steamer travel, and all the other superfluous appendages of life? To live in an atmosphere of victories to be, and to have already gained enough to convince me that others will surely come, is to make all so-called sacrifices of personal comforts no longer a task but a delight.

"FLORENCE, ITALY. My wife was informed by some Americans working here for the betterment of young women, that the Italian young women are now being set free to attend the universities and other educational institutions. They do not know what freedom means, and are in great danger because they have been restrained by rules and customs that held but did not instruct them. The young have not been allowed to mingle under proper guidance and example. They are not to blame, but the powers that have kept them thus uninformed are at fault. On the billboards here in Florence fine concerts are advertised to begin at twenty-one o'clock—they count time that way here. Think of it, the people going at bedtime to an entertainment to last several hours! Midnight is no time for amusement. It is the time when, among animals, only beasts of prey are roving about. This fact is of great significance, and should be noted in protecting our future citizens. It is the beast-of-prey part of any man that is most alert and seeking amusement at that late hour of the night. It is the time when the conscience is somewhat asleep and guardian parents are out of sight. It is the time when burglars, thieves, and highway robbers do their work. The moral villain knows full well when he can best operate. No sane person would blast the hope of a young life for a night's revelry if he realized the consequences."

The nation need not trouble about race-suicide. Let provision be ample to guard against race-degeneracy, and that will be enough. The strong race will reproduce; no fear about that. A sensible woman will not want a degenerate slave of tobacco, drink, or laziness for a life-companion and the father of her children; she will prefer to become a teacher, librarian, or typewriter. An intelligent, vigorous man will not want some slave of fashion or devotee of the card-table and the midnight dance as his companion and the mother of his children. Let the two strong, noble ones get sight of each other, and they will be drawn together by the mutual law of attraction that God has built into the very nature of them both. They must, however, first meet under proper conditions of mutual respect, and not of sudden familiarity of bodily caresses. This is a privilege of well-proved merit on either side, not a favor to be granted at sight. Two strong ones will unite and reproduce their kind. If they are weak, they can not be forever kept apart, but they will meet with a selfish animal-impulse, for pastime and indulgence. The spirit which says, "With that man or that woman as my life-companion I would be my best self," is entirely lacking. The weak young woman wants to meet the weak young man for what? Oh, he will buy her some chocolate or ice-cream, or take her to a dance or the theater. It will give her a chance to parade her fine clothes and make the other weaklings envious. The young man wants what? That varies. He may want a rich wife to support him in luxury and laziness; often his animal-nature is master, and he wants a young woman of attractive figure who is not too modest. The dance and the theater are places where modesty and morals are more frequently laughed at than honored, and he takes her there. They pass the time in a gay, free manner that robs each of something of respect for the other. Each of these two persons should find the chief attraction in noble companionship with a noble soul. Does life or eternity offer anything better than that? In the frivolities of life these two fail to find any enduring charm in each other. They each try another chance companion, and the same thing happens. Sometimes there is a deep sin, sometimes only the sin of trifling with the most important things of life, and thus spoiling life itself—and that is a serious matter.

"FLORENCE, April 27th. We went to Fiesole yesterday, where we had a very fine view of the valley of the Arno, and the mountains beyond. For a more extended view I climbed to the summit of the hill at the southeast. What impressed me most is the fact that at the summit, 1,500 feet high, there are extensive stone quarries. The workmen were friendly and cheerful at their hard and poorly-paid toil. I asked some questions, and went further, where I found a man working alone. He had a row of holes drilled in a large rock, and with wedges and a sledge-hammer he was splitting it. These men prepare window-sills, posts, or pavement-slabs, as the material will best serve. Florence is paved with large stone slabs. Near him were four healthy children, ranging from four to ten years old. They were playing quietly while the father plied his hammer rapidly to provide himself and family with very plain food and clothing. I used my little Italian as best I could in asking some questions, and then I told him he was helping to make the city beautiful with his work. He smiled, and hammered away as though no time were to be lost. I regarded his children for a little time with keen interest, then touched my hat to him as I gave him a cheerful parting salutation. I was compelled to say to myself that here is the nerve and sinew of Italy, and of every nation in the world. I take off my hat to them cheerfully, and thus I gather a wide sympathy with the people the world over who do the plain, necessary work.

I wound my way around the mountain, returning to the tram by another route. The women along the narrow streets were busy knitting, washing, sewing, or doing other useful work. The children played peacefully, and their mothers chatted merrily. I went into the curious old cathedral, which has lately been restored. Off in a side-chapel four or five priests of vigorous build were chanting some responsive service in a monotonous strain. There was no one to listen except one young woman, who appeared to be a tourist, trying to catch the words and learn what they were saying to themselves. I could catch no words, nor did I try very hard, as I knew it had nothing to do with the progress of Italy or of the world, both of which were of such intense interest to me.

We took the tram for Florence. Almost frequently enough to keep us constantly breathing their dust and vile fumes, we met one automobile after another going at insane speed. These fellows are the most selfish beings the world affords at present; they have no regard for the rights of others. I could not avoid some reflections on the way.

Perhaps human nature is no more selfish here than elsewhere, but the contrasts are sharper between the toiler who prepares the useful things of life and the idle class who seem to have little in their plans that benefits anybody whatsoever. Occasionally some fellow with a glib tongue gets tired breaking stone or some other work; he finds it easier to labor with his mouth, and turns agitator. He tells the workmen how they are abused, points to the selfish use of money that is most evident, and sooner or later there is a strike or a labor-war of some kind. I believe the worst way to begin a reform is to set employers and employed to fighting each other. War-methods have always been bad, and will never be good. The patience of millions of the faithful toilers the world over is commendable. Those in plenty and in power should get down on their knees in just acknowledgment of their wrong dealing with this class. They may not do that; they will not in large numbers, unless compelled to, which I hope may never be necessary. It is surely not too much to ask them to waste less on luxuries, and help the children of these toilers to the training and education that will lift them out of the reach of agitators and other enemies of progress. Labor-wars and strikes cost too much in money, time, and good-will. No one will deny that in connection with strikes, better conditions have come to laborers; but that does not prove that more would not have been accomplished by studying out the real fault, finding those to blame, and then applying reasoning methods and fostering a spirit of friendship. It certainly is the duty of those who are able to visit different parts of the world and observe the varied conditions, to gather the best from all sources and apply it to the benefit of the general welfare. Italy has good material for a great people. May the spirit of her toilers who labor patiently on to support their families, rule that land; and not the spirit of the idle pleasure-seekers, indifferent to all but themselves!"

THE NATION AND SELF-MASTERY

One great need of the countries in Southern Europe is a genuine respect for woman. Artists have searched the country for beautiful women to serve as nude models in sculpture and painting. It is a degradation of womankind to treat her in this way. Her true virtues do not appear in the least in the average product. When woman is to be truthfully represented, she is not put up without clothing; we have always seen our mothers and all our useful women properly clad. We have read of naked savages; but they know no better. In these countries, where in art woman is so often represented as a handsome animal, she is thought of as such in a large degree. No woman can long continue to be what artists call handsome, and have her spiritual, mental, and physical powers developed. Character, mental growth, and physical service all make lines on the face and person. Motherhood must yield something of her beauty as a necessary sacrifice to usefulness, but it reappears in her offspring.

This kind of art makes the fatal blunder of placing woman's greatest charms below her chin. It tends to animal-mastery in men, and women too. Spiritual mastery on the part of both sexes is the only thing that can give woman her true place of honor and respect. The art that can not live without feeding on naked women had better starve to death; that portion can well be spared. Very wisely the laws of America prevent the sale or display of obscene pictures. That same law, if consistently enforced, would rid the galleries of much that is just as bad, but by tradition from pagan times has been dignified with the name of art. If it is necessary to civilization that people should wear clothes, then it is bad to see representations of their unclad forms on canvas or in stone. We who have studied human nature know that the average man has battle enough with himself to keep his thoughts where they should be, without adding any special fuel to the fires which already rage too fiercely within him at times.

There are those who will ask why I mention the Roman hierarchy in this connection. My answer is, that, knowing the past history and the present policy of the Vatican, it is impossible to be loyal to our country and a friend to the childhood of the world, and be silent on the conduct of papal Rome toward our own children and neighbors and toward the vital interests of every country. I do not attack the Catholic Church; on the contrary, I have confidence in its powers for good, I believe it has a great future, and I am working to hasten the day of justice and freedom to its millions of faithful people.

Here is the vital point at issue. I insist that the little group of high officials at Rome, which calls itself the head of the church, is not a necessary or even useful part of it, but is a hindrance to the best interests of the whole body of the Catholic Church, and to humanity in general. Separate the two, and one will easily see that the body will gain immensely without such a head. If the Catholic people in every country will cease to take commands from Rome, will open their minds to the truth from all sources, and then will follow their own best judgment, the cause of childhood and the interests of humanity the world over will move forward surprisingly. If any one thinks the Catholic people with their clergy could not manage all their affairs in America better without the interference of the Vatican, he must place them far below their true rank of intelligence. My attitude toward that church is that those people have the ability to direct their religious activities far better when they are free to follow the dictates of their own understanding and the needs of the people.

The strength of the Roman Hierarchy lies in its intensely concentrated organization. The higher officials are elderly men, behind whom the bridges have been burned, and those following fill the ranks of succession and prevent return. At their head is a man thoroughly in love with power, with the homage of his followers, and with the glitter of high office, and who is so old that his stiffened spiritual and mental joints can not bend. This great central power is entirely out of the reach of the people and the real vigor of the church, and is strong because of isolation. The children, before they know their right hand from their left, are taught to make their religious belief include the right of the Vatican to rule them. Mohammedanism fastens its vices on the people by the same principle of impressing the mind of the child. I am not speaking of the Catholic Church in general, that consists in each country of the people with their clergy, I speak only of that little group of high officials in Rome, which is no part of the real church, but simply a foreign parasite on its life. This same Vatican is the prime cause of illiteracy and backwardness in Italy, in all the Latin countries, and especially in the Latin Americas.

Any future pope will have in his power the possibility of making himself the most distinguished of the whole papal line if he will open the Bible to the people, set the priesthood free to follow their own best judgment regarding marriage and local government, and cut loose from the pernicious traditions of the Dark Ages. To help him take this step becomes the important duty of all who are outside of that church, and thus they will aid in liberating its millions from a bondage which has endured far too long. This is not so much a religious question, nor is it simply a local question: it is of national and international importance; it is a problem of all humanity whether some arbitrary power or any selfish interest shall interfere with the best education of the young and prejudice the minds of children against their companions and neighbors. The interference of a foreign power with the education of the children of America, in the selfish interests of that same foreign power, works a benefit to no one, and is an incalculable wrong to the childhood of America and of the world.

A WORLD-NEIGHBORHOOD.

Each nation should regard itself as an individual among other nations and bound to keep the Golden Rule with its neighbors. Like an individual, it must not shoot across the border, menace the peace by carrying weapons, nor send its criminals and paupers into its neighbor's territory. It must police itself, support itself, and pension itself. It is a family in a larger world-neighborhood, and as such is bound by the same laws of honesty, peace, and friendship that holds any family in a well-regulated Christian community.

THE NATION AND WORLD-RESOURCES.

The supplies of timber, coal, iron, and many other products of the earth are world-supplies, and should be regarded as such; they are necessities of civilization, and the quantity of each is limited. It is a matter of importance, therefore, whether any nation or any individual wastes these items of wealth. It is a national question whether a few persons have the right to consume large amounts of lumber in building mansions, and then to burn an unusual amount of fuel in heating them; whether people have any right to exhaust the supply of gasoline in pleasure-rides, when that same material is needed for doing useful work; whether any one may rightfully consume on his pleasures what the community needs for its necessities. Holding the key to the public treasury does not give one the right to waste its contents on himself; holding the deeds to the timber and mining-lands does not give one the right to squander on himself what God has placed there for all the people and for all time. We who live now, owe it to our children to leave the earth a garden rather than a desert. It becomes our imperative duty to husband the mineral wealth of the world and develop and conserve the fruitfulness of the soil in the interests of each nation, in the interests of the whole family of nations, and for the welfare of the future race of mankind.

CHAPTER VIII

THE HOME AND SELF-MASTERY

WE all desire a great nation. The first essential for this is strong, intelligent, individual men and women. To produce strong men and women, a good home is necessary; and to have a good home, its rights and privileges must be guarded against all enemies. Destroy the nesting-place of birds, and soon the flock will disappear; protect them in their nesting-time and place, and the mature birds will care for themselves. Man is like the birds in this, except that the simple life and rapid development of the birds require protection but for a brief period. Man is complex, the period of youth and development is long, and his nesting-time is greatly extended. All that is necessary for his nest is two or more plainly-furnished rooms, with an income reasonably certain, and sufficient for sensible needs. The personal equipment is a vigorous, manly man and a vigorous, womanly woman, who prefer each other as life-companions to any one else. The neighbors may think it a misfit, but if the two are satisfied, they have eternal rights to be let alone, and to be helped, not hindered, in their home-building aspirations.

The work of the home is to build great men and women. Whatever improves the man, or the woman, or the home, improves the nation; whatever injures the man, or the woman, or the home, injures the nation. A defect in any of these is a serious matter. A defective father, a defective mother, or a defective home will surely stamp some defect on the young citizen.

God has provided men and women with qualities and

140

mutual attractions which draw the two together for mutual benefit. These two persons form a companionship and a co-operative union for life. When they have been properly born of good parents and trained in good homes, a successful and happy union is within easy reach. For such a successful union each must seek to cultivate and retain all natural and acquired graces and attractions. Whatever robs either man or woman of these graces and attractions, without giving in its place a better substitute, is bad for the man, bad for the woman, bad for the home, bad for the children, and bad for the community. Each must strive to respect fully the other's personal rights and the rights of the home. If one injures the fibers that are to compose a rope, he injures the finished rope. The man and the woman and the home, with the several rights of each, twisted into strands, and then into the combined product, make the rope on which hangs the destiny of the nation.

It is well to bear in mind the fact that the home which produces the most excellent men and women is the one that brings the greatest happiness to all its inmates. Such a home is a good neighbor, should this and another home choose to unite some of its younger members in marriage. Doubtless there will always be a few of both sexes who, for some reason, will travel life's pathway without the matrimonial degree; but these will be few in that day when the home comes into possession of all its rights. Let a million baby boys and a million baby girls be born in this country in a period of years. Let each be well-born, and let them all be trained into strong, manly men and womanly women. Let them mingle under proper conditions of society, in the homes, churches, schools, and clean recreation and wholesome amusement, and there will be an exceedingly small number of these who will not find a congenial companion somewhere and for life. The divorce-courts and scandal-mongers will be able to take a twelve-month's vacation every year.

THE AIM OF THE HOME.

The highest aim of the home is to produce the best individual men and women. When all the rights of the home are restored to it, and when complete justice is rendered to the child, before and after birth, it will be easy to see that man was made in the image of his Maker. Let us take one man and one woman at their best, fresh and new, in the morning of life. Comparing the one with the other, perhaps they are not equal in anything; they are different, but they are just and fair in everything. Plainly one standard of habits and morals must serve for both. Neither has any right to be selfish, or to ask privileges that are not allowed to both. It is a great privilege for both to say, our home, our common interests, our children, our joys or sorrows. Each can say of the other, My companion believes in me, prefers me to all others, represents my better self, shares my sorrows and rejoices at my success. These two, in partnership with God, can endure the world or defy the world, as the case may require. Concerning their children, it is not so easy a problem. Bad neighbors and bad company crowd in upon the rights of the best homes and hinder their work. There are enough good homes in this country to prove fully the possibility of having all homes of that class, homes where the husband and wife each measure up to a high standard, and the children likewise. It may be objected that a few instances do not prove the possibility of all; that it is easier to hit a target one time out of five than to hit it every time. My answer is, Do away with the distance between you and the target, and you can hit it every time; remove its enemies, and bring in its friends, and you can have a good home every time.

THE FRIENDS OF THE HOME.

God is the first and greatest friend of the home; where He rules, peace and happiness abide.

The Bible is the friend of the home; it is ever a safe and helpful counselor, imparting wisdom to every member of the household.

The Christian Church is a friend of the home, where neighbors may mingle under the best conditions of fellowship and mutual helpfulness.

If Christ and His religion are fully installed in any home, its own individual needs will sooner or later be all provided for. This does not make the neighborhood safe, unless all the other homes are also Christian. It is often asked, Why are not all the children in certain good homes of an upright character? The answer might be, Because they have had bad neighbors. Missionaries in heathen lands feel this most of all, as their young children are in great danger from the outside influences. There are too many heathen in all lands. They come and entice the children from good homes into folly and sin on the delusive plea of having a good time.

THE ENEMIES OF THE HOME.

The saloon and intoxicating liquor in every form are fatal to the best interests of the home. They brutalize the people and squander the money needed for the household.

Tobacco wastes the money that is needed for food, clothing, and books. It makes the air vile and unfit to breathe, and, in its particular sphere, it makes beasts out of otherwise good men. I believe its devotees would vote tobacco out of use by a vast majority if they could thus be freed from its mastery over themselves.

Gambling and the games that lead to gambling and dishonesty; prostitution and the amusements which lead in that direction, especially the dance and theater, are enemies of the home.

This includes the clubs which take any members away from the home when they are needed there. This means the older members, if they are needed to care for others, or the young people who ought to spend more time at home and make it bright for parents who have done so much for them. Neither is to be selfish, but parents have some rights to the society of grown-up children during part of their evening and leisure hours.

Anything that helps the young to reach the age of manhood and womanhood with all their powers well preserved and developed is a friend to the home.

Anything that lowers the grade of their manhood and womanhood, or deprives them of qualities needed for parenthood, is an enemy of the home.

WOMAN AND SELF-MASTERY.

One of the greatest needs of the present time in the movement for a higher type of humanity is that full justice and respect be meted out to the womanhood of the world. There can be no exceptions made to this rule concerning any race or occupation. It is not equality that is to be sought—the two sexes, man and woman, are not equal, and never can be. They are unequal in looks, in strength, in the possibility of personal wrong, and in the capacity for self-defense. They are unequal in the strength of the temptation which leads to immorality. They are unequal in the suffering from the effects of the sin of immorality in which both engage. God made the man to be the father, and the woman to be the mother of the race. This of necessity makes them unequal in all that pertains to the more immediate and vital concerns of parenthood. Neither can perform the duties of the other, neither can shirk his own duty without great loss, but each can give a full measure of justice and respect to the other. God made men and women not to be equal and the same, but that each should be the perfect complement of the other. The two, living and working in a close companionship, should form a union which, moving in harmony with God, lacks nothing that can be desired.

The greatest failure of the race up to the present time has been the failure of the men and the women in possession of intelligence and power to do justice to the womanhood of the world. The first great duty to the unborn and the undeveloped children is to see that the motherhood of the race be no longer dwarfed and enslaved. The womanhood of the world must be made free from the slavery of man's unmastered lust, from the slavery of pernicious fashion in dress and customs of modern society, and from any slavery made potent by false religion and tradition.

The bane of all heathen religions is the debasement of woman on alleged religious grounds. The teaching and practice of Confucianism, of Buddhism, of Mohammedanism, and of Mormonism definitely require or sanction the partial degradation of woman. Even that branch of Christianity which has made the loudest and most belligerent claims of divine origin and authority, has degraded woman by its claim that the clergy can be better servants of God and man if forbidden the companionship of woman as life-partner in marriage. This implies, at least, that to become his wife and the mother of his children, and thus to furnish for him a home and all that that means in the way of influence for good, a woman would interfere with his highest usefulness in the redemption of the race. This is an injustice to woman, a wrong of the deepest dye against all the clergy of that church, and seriously interferes with the harmonious working of the various denominations of Christians. The world well knows that no man desirous of keeping himself unspotted from sin, ever found the companionship of a true wife, to whom he himself was also true, other than a help, and not a hindrance, to his own virtue and manhood. The celibacy required by the Vatican rulers in the church does not rest on religious grounds at all, but on the determination of those rulers to hold all Christendom in their power. It is for this they require men and women, connected with the direct work of the Church, to take vows not to marry. Opposition to the law of celibacy is in no sense or degree an attack on the Catholic Church, but rather an act of kindness in relieving a multitude of people, in many lands, from a pernicious tradition that has caused untold harm to civilization in general, and to womanhood in particular. The intelligent women of the world should unite to free their sisters from a traditional despotism, which, because of being linked with the religion of a great church, is like a huge monster holding its victim powerless in its grasp.

Licentiousness is mainly the sin of the man, yet its penalties fall heaviest on woman. The man may usually reform and recover his place in respectable company; not so the woman. If man would even recognize to himself the harm he does to woman in this sin, it would be a most powerful aid to him in resisting his own temptation to ruin the life of one in his power. The mothers and older sisters have one important field open to them for cultivation. It is the minds and thoughts of the boys that need to be trained intelligently to appreciate the mental and spiritual, rather than the physical attractions of girls and women. If women knew the terrible strain of the temptation that disturbs the peace of many youths and older men, they would be more careful to guard the approaches to this temptation.

Alcoholic Liquor.—Alcoholic liquor, in all its aspects and customs as a beverage, is a great enemy of woman. It hardens the heart of her father, her husband, her son, and her neighbor against her. It squanders the money that belongs to her, and even that which her own hands have earned, and which is sorely needed for bread and clothing. It takes away the society of father, husband, or son on many an evening that should be spent at home, helping to perform its duties, and make its prospects brighter.

Tobacco.—Tobacco is also an enemy of woman. The men of her household who use it are always more or less enslaved by this expensive, filthy habit. It defiles the air she must breathe, often in cramped quarters; it weakens her offspring through a weakened fatherhood; it injures the children by compelling them in infancy to breathe strong fumes of poisoned air. It consumes the money of the family purse; it hardens the hearts of the men who should bethink themselves more for human betterment. There comes a lack in the home, the husband knows it, and is disturbed by it. He takes a smoke or chew of tobacco, and the prodding of his conscience to bestir himself is blunted, and he goes on without the needed improvement. It will be objected that this is not true in every case. It is not apparent in every case, but had it not been for the benumbing effects of liquor and tobacco on the large number of men who *do care* for better things, the rights of women would have been attended to long before a few of them began to do foolish things to gain those rights. It can be asked, what could make some good men so selfish as to have them compel their attractive, clean wives and daughters to endure their tobacco smoke and breath? The answer is, nothing except tobacco could do that, but tobacco can and does. It first enslaves a man, and then dulls his sense of wrong to his best friends.

War. — War is always and everywhere an enemy of woman. If the words were written in blood, it would be impossible to describe the wrongs and suffering that war has brought upon woman in the world's history. In this aspect of war there is no excuse that can be offered, there is no justification that can be made. The selfishness and brutality which are so magnified in war are manifested toward woman, and help to make man's nature less amenable to justice and reason. War tends to decide questions of disagreement by force, rather than by an appeal to reason and fair play. The wrong and injustice of war to womankind, if there were no other argument against it, is a sufficient cause for its abolition.

The Dance and Theater are the enemies of woman inasmuch as they arouse the animal nature in man. They do not emphasize the spiritual and the mental excellence of woman, but rather her physical attraction. The dominance of the spirit and the intellect makes lines in the face and renders the form less attractive. It is the round, plump figure of a young woman that is most alluring in the theater and dance. This too often catches evil eyes of husbands who have more money than principle, and broken homes and broken hearts are the results. Of many a comely young woman it can be said, her face and her form were her misfortune. And it was the avenue of sesuous amusements by which the spoiler entered who wrecked her life. The theater or the dance brought the two together, the victim within striking distance of the villain.

To-day the papers contained an account of a French woman of some note shooting an American. Both were married, and the American woman had gotten the husband of the French woman away from her. The latter had appealed to her to desist, and not ruin her home and happiness. This time she went to her and begged her to cease. The American said coldly, "I have gotten your husband, and I intend to keep him." Then the other fired two shots and killed her. Following this she went to the police and gave herself up, telling how she had suffered from the crimes of that woman. The French woman deserves our sincere sympathy. Society is to blame for condoning such crimes as that American woman was guilty of. She was a traitor to God, to the State, and to three people at least—the two husbands and the wife. Yet idle, over-fed, rich society plays at that diabolical game just for fun. The dance and the theater tend in the direction of all such crimes, and help make a plaything of woman and affection, thus corrupting both. Woman has a higher destiny, oh! that she might make a greater effort herself, and have more help from man to find it!

No one can make a rope out of sand, nor a cement wall of hemp. The sand can be made into cement, and the hemp into rope; that was the plan of the Creator, and it can not be changed. Likewise, the Creator has given woman her place, and she must be permitted to fill that place according to His plan. She must be in possession of her own peculiar reserve power. She must have a strong individual identity, and never yield the citadel of her own personal privileges to any intruder. She is primarily the queen of the home, the wife and companion of man, and the mother of the race. Man must have mother, sister, wife and daughter. He must have a circle of womanly friends who trust, respect, and inspire him to be his best self at all times. Woman can not retain her true position in man's regard and be his toy. The soft, low-voiced gem of the Oriental harem may pass for the Mohammedan, but educated Christian manhood desires something more definitely individual.

It would be a surprise to know how much is lost to womanhood, because the genuine worth of so many women is obscured by unduly expensive clothing. A friend of mine gave me this experience which I repeat almost in his own words:

"I had a real fright at the beginning of my serious acquaintance with the one who afterwards became my wife. I had been invited to her home for the evening. I had entered, and stood talking for a moment, when the approach of rustling silk startled me. I looked up and caught my breath. It was the young woman I had set my sails to catch, if all went well. My heart sank as the thought came to me that I could not bind myself to furnish wind for sails of that quality. I learned later that the silken rustle was not the measure of the girl's good sense; but I might not have learned it until too late. Now, after years of acquaintance, I know that my wife is sensible about dress."

This is not a rare instance; there are many excellent young men and women who would join fortunes in good homes if it were not that the young man feels he can not guarantee her such clothes as she now wears, and yet she wears them to look attractive to him. It is a mistaken opinion that each has of the other. It is too often the fine apparel that hides the real worth of the woman in the eyes of a worthy young man. Many, at heart, are sensible about dress, and if they were joined to some industrious young man they would do their part in the frequent needs of economy while getting started in life. The worthless young men are not frightened away by fine clothes; they do not care, they may hope to be supported by a rich wife. They will take the chances, and if life goes hard they quit. It is the better grade of young men who will not ask a woman to dress more plainly for them, or risk compelling them to do so. Pretty faces and fine garments are in reach of but few, nor do they long give their possessor the power she covets. She must have strength and skill, both in hands and brain. These are the charms and virtues that endure, and keep woman in her own queenly realm all the way through life.

Oh, ye men and women who are blessed with happy homes, and live in the joy and benefit of an honored womanhood, would that I might take you with me to see the faithfulness of the millions of toiling women in the less favored parts of the earth! In Africa, in Asia, in Mexico, in the southern Americas, woman is loyally trying to do her part. There is a vast number of them of whom it can be said personally, as Christ said of one, "She hath done what she could." She has done her best under her cramped circumstances.

Far too often religion has furnished the excuse for her degradation. This must be said to the shame of the higher officials of every form of religion that sanctions the debasement of woman in any degree. Omitting names and places, the following comes from my own experience: A certain church official very kindly escorted me to visit a boys' school of which he was justly proud. All the appointments were commendable. The efficiency of the school was largely due to the ability and devotion of the head teacher. Judge of my surprise as we approached, to see that same dignified woman drop on her knee, kiss his hand, and address him in terms of marked superiority. I was ashamed of the man who would allow such a teacher to show him subjection in the name of religion before those boys ; while he seemed only pleased with it all. I have the fullest respect for that man as a man, and for that woman as a woman. It is the tyranny of tradition that rules them both, and, worst of all, it teaches the children a false and pernicious doctrine in reference to woman's true place in the world.

CHAPTER IX

AMUSEMENTS AND SELF-MASTERY

RECREATION and amusements have a vital connection with the work of training the young, and it is very important that boys and girls should become masters of themselves in this department. People are saying to-day, Young people must have amusement. That puts the emphasis in the wrong place. That they become strong, true men and women is the goal to be reached, and we must conduct them to that goal by the best route. It is a serious question whether we have any time or need for amusement, unless it practically means recreation. It is re-creation, however, that is needed. This is a field that should be studied far more than it has been in the past; it has been left too much to chance, and to those who are eager to make money without hard work. This matter needs the best direction it can have from the combined wisdom of education, religion, business and science. Some amusements do not pay, there is a better way to spend time and money; some are harmful to health and morals, and some are not right between man and man.

Children need to be taught how to amuse themselves, they need to be instructed in the art of recreation. It is a very easy matter for several or even two intelligent young people to find wholesome recreation if they know how. The dance, gambling cards, and the theater tend to make people dependent and helpless in the matter of providing their own amusements. If one gets into either of these ruts it is hard to get out, they shut off originality. It becomes simply a question of money and time to go and be amused by falling into line with whatever these may offer. There are many games with other than gambling cards that have not been spoiled by the professionals. Intelligence can enjoy them, and can invent more when these fail or tire. Like a good appetite for plain, wholesome food, a keen relish for simple, spontaneous recreation can be so cultivated as to give entire satisfaction. The people must be trained and equipped from childhood to provide their own recreation and amusement of a beneficial and not injurious or expensive nature.

The drama can be utilized in the home as an attraction. People can read the parts, or learn them as they choose. It is only the person of weak mind who needs such elaborate and barbarously expensive trappings as some theaters have. The imagination of an intelligent person can supply all that is needed beyond moderate equipment. The love of applause on the stage pushes a crowd of young people into dangerous ventures, and they in turn create a craze for amusement which draws a large following, and thus the blind lead the blind into the ditch of expensive and degrading amusements. Those who have jaded and worn out their own sensibilities with a surfeit of amusement may need something extreme to arouse their interest. Pagan Rome became so callous to ordinary amusements that no play murder would satisfy, it must be real. We are in danger in that same direction; character, at least, is too often murdered.

There seem to be a great many young men and women, even college-bred, who are so callous to each other's charms that they are not satisfied with an evening together in conversation, music, and intellectual games. They seem to be incapable of finding sufficient pleasure in each other's company at a little distance, they have to get into bodily contact. If the animal nature has to come in to that extent, the intellectual must be blunted indeed. That is the type of the savage whose mind is not developed. I am sure the possibilities of enjoyment of both sexes is far greater without the excesses of late hours and such intimacy as the dance permits and requires. The higher nature and sensibilities need to be cultivated. Intelligent young people, properly taught, can enjoy each other's society without getting their hands on each other. Each has a native charm for the other which is rubbed off by contact. Animals could not enjoy an art gallery, they must come in touch with everything. So must persons whose more delicate sensibilities have been worn out. That is why those who have become enamored with these three forms of amusement can rarely be led to enjoy any other—everything else is too tame.

It is certain that intelligent people can find abundant amusements that are within easy reach of the multitude that are not expensive, and are far removed from danger either to health or morals. In our own family and many others I have known, there have always been more ways of recreation than there was time for. It can be so in every case where intelligence has kept out excesses and directed the energies wisely,

RECREATION IN WORK.

If all those engaged in useful employment had the true conception of their calling, namely, that they are engaged in that work because they want to support themselves and do their part in the world, the very joy of usefulness would have a large measure of recreative power for them while they are at their daily tasks. Children work hard at their play and enjoy it; when they are properly taught they will learn to play hard at their work and enjoy that also. The past has blundered badly in honoring and envying the idle, worthless nabob, and in scorning the useful toiler. Too many talk as though all the year were drudgery except the few weeks of vacation. One can make it so for himself, but that is a sad perversion of life's best opportunities.

One important principle has been overlooked in this field. It is that every wholesome amusement can be participated in by all ages, old and young together, by those who care to join. If anything looks silly or out of place for an old person who is active enough to take part in it, the thing is wrong, or the taste that condemns it is wrong. One must weigh diamonds with delicate scales; the way to detect any subtle evil is with delicate tests. If any amusement has to be carefully guarded as to the place where it is allowed, or concerning the persons who may engage in it, these tests condemn that amusement for all. It is a bad man, it is a bad woman, who can not be trusted to move freely among the old and the young, the strong and the weak, the rich and the poor, wherever common humanity are found, without taking advantage of them or influencing them to their hurt. It is a bad amusement that can not be left free to take its own natural course among the old and the young, the strong and the weak, the rich and the poor, wherever common humanity are found, without injuring the young people eager for fun, but ignorant of danger, and not able to protect themselves.

To say some certain amusement does not hurt me, usually means that one does not feel any sudden shock or is not immediately disabled by it. As well might one drink a dose of poison and say it did not hurt him, before it had had time to take effect. How can boys or girls of sixteen know whether a thing hurts them or not, when the harm does not show for several years? I have had my pupils tell me it did not hurt them to do this or that, and that they could get their lessons just as well, when, at the time of their examination, it came out very plainly that they had been hurt and they could not do as well. Later in life, when it was past recall, the evidence was strong enough to be seen even by one who all the time was trying not to see it. Such weighty matters can not be left to inexperience; older heads must decide all such questions.

There are those who say, let each one follow his own conscience in regard to amusements. Paul did that in persecuting the Christians, but he found later that he was following a falsely educated conscience. The young person could follow his conscience in choosing which of several roads to take in traveling through a strange country as safely as he could follow that same guide in choosing the right path among the many ways, good and bad, which are open to him in life's journey. The safe way through a forest, and the safe way through life, are matters of knowledge, not of conscience. Too many override their conscience and follow their inclination, even when they have some misgivings about certain things. It is so easy for one to stifle that voice within him, and defy his own better judgment, that the only safe rule is for each to refuse himself permission to do in his own sphere whatever will be dangerous for the common throng to do in theirs. These are my children, and my younger brothers and sisters; whatever hurts them in their sphere hurts me in mine. King David, though a warrior, would not drink the water from the spring at Bethlehem, because the three men had gotten it in jeopardy of their lives, and to drink that water, he said, would be drinking their blood. There are a multitude of good people who are practically drinking the blood of thousands of young men and girls whose characters and lives are being sacrificed in supplying the amusements in which these good, comfortable people indulge. If I were to become so callous as not to care whether these were injured or not, my susceptibilities to the finer joys of life would be so blunted that the world I live in would become insipid to me, and I should have to move down among the coarser animal pleasures whose days soon end in ruin. I get more joy, yes, more pleasure, out of being my brother's keeper—and my Lord's companion—than I can believe any person gets out of questionable amusements, when all the years of life from six to sixty are counted.

A MISTAKE IN ATHLETICS.

Amusements have become too artificial and unnatural, and they are dwarfing the people's ability to provide their own recreation. Children can have too many toys and too little chance to think out their own sports and games. There is a natural inventive genius in man, and an instinct of play, and these, coupled with the desire of children to do whatever they see others doing, would, under wise direction, finally lead all the people, old and young, to join in simple, wholesome, and entirely helpful sports and pastimes. Body, mind and spirit would be benefited, and the animal instinct in man would be directed into useful energy, instead of being perverted into the channels of excess and immorality.

Another very serious mistake that has been made in the field of recreation is that athletics have almost entirely deserted their true sphere, and have entered that of the show business. Football, basket ball, and baseball have gone out of the hands of the masses who need exercise, into the hands of a few picked Samsons who need such drill least of all. Where ten or twenty experts perform in the ring, and several thousand merely look on and howl themselves hoarse, the performers might as well be monkeys, dogs, or Mexican bull fighters, so far as any physical training for the multitude is concerned. It is not necessary to go to college to be taught to shout one's self hoarse at some trivial victory of one college "dozen" over another college "dozen" in a ball game. It is a mark of savagery to go to such extremes of enthusiasm to defeat another, or over another's defeat—and all just for fun. If it were to defeat the liquor traffic or the tobacco habit, clean up politics, or even for a genuine reform in spelling English, all might join the crowd and shout for the victors with energy.

The showmen are teaching the children and youth the show habit, and thus leading them to spend their money foolishly, and at the same time making them helpless and unable to provide their own amusement. All that is beneficial in this field could be provided through far more wholesome channels. If the whole tribe of these showmen who are running the theaters, shows, dances, and professional ball-playing were colonized on farms where they would become useful producers instead of corrupting the young people, the world would gain immensely thereby.

I repeat the complaint that professionals have taken athletics away from the masses who need them, and degraded nearly the whole affair into a show business for money. I want to play ball myself for my own benefit. I want to catch the fire of younger enthusiasm in their midst as one of them. Meanwhile, I see the other players and cheer them on, and they cheer me, and all with mutual benefit. We might as well pay a few experts to do our eating for us simply because they could beat us on the time and quantity test. We need exercise and we need food, why should we hire experts to do our ball-playing, any more than to do our eating? I believe it is bad tradition from pagan times that spoils athletics to-day. It is high time to retire pagan tradition from several fields of modern activity.

SHOULD BE CENSORED.

Every amusement or recreation ought to be required to pass through four screens before being allowed to be taught to the coming generation:

1. Education. Is its teaching helpful and not harmful in its general bearing on the young?

2. Science. Is it beneficial to health and to physical and mental development?

3. Business. Does it pay? Is it too expensive? Does it lead people to spend money for what they can not afford?

4. Religion. Is it right? Is it an enemy or rival of the home? Does it offer any perils to chaste young womanhood and manhood? Would it be entirely proper for the best men and women, for teachers, ministers, fathers and mothers to participate in it, both as actors and as observers, at the times and places where it is left free to take its own course?

There are surely enough games, pastimes, and entertainments that can stand these tests with a clean and unanimous commendation, to furnish all the recreation and amusement that people have time for, or can use with profit. It is very important that the best scientific, religious, educational, and business talent be turned to the study of so important a subject as this. Science and common sense are working together to keep injurious and unwholesome ingredients out of our food. There is no more reason for having injurious or even questionable elements in our amusements than there is for having them in our food. The play and recreation influences and agencies count very much in the issues of life; they hold the switch that turns many a person on the sidetrack of ruin, or sends him on the main line to success and noble achievement.

THE DANCE AND THE HOME.

Inasmuch as the dance is taking such a prominent place in society, and in our high schools, normal schools, colleges and universities, I have, as a study, personified this amusement and presented the case as an interview between Mr. Dance and Mr. Home. Let those dispute my conclusions who have traveled further and studied the problems of youth and the home more thoroughly than I have.

"Good morning, Mr. Home, my name is Dance; I see you have some attractive sons and daughters and I have called to offer my services to yourself and family."

"Yes, Mr. Dance, I have heard of you frequently. You may present your claims and recommendations, I will hear your story from yourself."

"Mr. Home, you may know that I have customers in all ranks of society from the highest to the lowest. In the palaces of kings and emperors, and in the habitations of the humble workman, I am found. The rich and the poor, the great and the small, the good and the bad, I count among my customers. I am cosmopolitan, I am very broad and liberal, I am admired in colleges and universities, and in the camps of savages. I serve all who wish me day or night, and I should be glad to be at your disposal at any time or place. I am admitted to every place except the church, and one or two denominations of very respectable people sometimes build a dance-hall adjoining the church, and, judging by their conduct, they seem to be much happier there in my service than in the church itself. Some churches condemn me and call me bad, but I get a good many of their young people away from them, and some of the frisky older ones also. I can give one privilege that even parents can not furnish. I can introduce a man and woman on the dance floor, and they will fall into each other's arms as though they were affianced lovers, and swing around until they are tired. No other power can grant such liberty to respectable people with no guarantee of character on the part of either."

"Mr. Dance, I am interested in your statement. You certainly have a wide range of customers; you seem to be about as widely distributed as sin. You appear to be welcome wherever sin is admitted, perhaps you two are in partnership. I have heard of you from my childhood days. My parents told me about you, and my church and Sunday school also gave me instructions concerning your work and influence. While I was at the university, and under circumstances where you could appear at your very best, I made your more intimate acquaintance. I saw you at the extreme end of your course farthest removed from your worst features. Since that time I have studied your work and influence systematically in all its various phases. I do not speak as a novice, but from long acquaintance with you and your friends.

"Now, let me tell you who I am. My name is Christian Home; I am employed by the firm of God and Humanity. I represent them, work for them, and do my best for them in all possible ways. The firm I represent has the entire care and responsibility for the birth, education, development and eternal welfare of every child born into this world. One single defective child or person, of any color or in any clime, reflects some degree of reproach on the firm. So you see we are interested in all those people whom you count as your customers. I have taken employment with this firm, not only as a trusted business agent, but, in addition to this, I have taken a vow, of the most solemn nature, of faithfulness for life and eternity. I have invested my money in the firm, and I have taken my family with me, so you will see I am very closely bound up with all their interests.

"You represent a firm that is a sworn enemy of ours. I am obliged to speak and act very frankly and firmly with all who wish to deal with the people, or serve in their homes. I am vitally interested in the influences that shape the lives of the young people. I shall speak plainly, and tell you what I know you to be. I will simply act as a mirror for you. First of all, you are always a substitute for something better than yourself. No place is too low or degraded for you. You enter the bad resorts and make them worse. You are most at home, and feel the freest in dives, saloons and brothels; in fact you are so vile that the laws in some cities will not allow you even in the saloons, because you ruin so many young girls, and of course you ruin the men also.

"You are a thief because you steal the hearts, the tender affection and the attention of husbands and wives, and bestow them on the chance partner of the time and place. Often these are men and women who are well dressed and have outside polish, but who are of the lowest possible character. You are the cause of divorce in a large number of instances. Married persons meet another at a dance, where at the midnight hours you give permission of 'free hugging for all' on the bare recommendation of an introduction for the evening. These two persons may know nothing of each other beyond this, nor be expected to recognize each other the next day on the street. The sentiment 'be mine for an hour' prevails in the dance. This leads to flirtation, to playing at making love, and as there is a kind of ecstasy and rapture in the close bodily contact of the sexes, one or both begin to feel that a mistake has been made in getting married—the wrong life partner has been taken, there would be greater happiness with this one. If that is possibly true, this fact better never be known when it is too late to change. You are to blame for telling the foolish people after it is too late. Usually it is not true, and here is the fault. Each compares this chance partner at a midnight frolic with the husband or wife at home in the humdrum duties of necessary work, and the contrast is unfair and deceptive.

"Again, you rob the home and married life of what are its exclusive privileges. You allow two persons, a man and a woman, who are not related, to be very familiar and confidential in the midnight hours, to hold each other's hands, to embrace each other, and to act for the time as though they were life companions. These are the exclusive privileges of two who are married to each other, or expecting soon to be. You give these privileges to the young before their time, and thus they wear out in frolics that freshness of each which is intended to last as an attraction for the home and marriage during a lifetime. These charms were intended to keep husband and wife true to each other and satisfied with each other for a whole life, and you make them common and wear them out in the excesses of a few years of youth when they are not needed. Many do not marry because they can get, as they think, all the privileges of married life they seek, simply for money, through the help of the dance. Of course they are deceived, for you give them only the coarser animal pleasures.

"Without you, it would be impossible for the bad ones to get acquainted with many of their victims, and to come within striking distance of them. With many others there is no intention of sin, but they are led up to it by the arousing of the tiger in the animal part of man's nature, which is a perilous matter. Many, very many do not break any definite law, and think they do no harm to themselves or to the other. They do not know that you rob both of them of that delicate charm which God gave to each sex in the sight of the other—of that charm which makes marriage and home life so happy in multitudes of cases where such liberties with the other sex have never been taken. Yet you do rob them, and you deny having done it. You rob the parents of the society of their young people in the evening hours, and leave the home lonesome. You rob the night of its quiet and rest. You do most of your work after bedtime for busy people. You rob the man of the love, confidence and society of his wife on many nights, or the greater part of the night, and the same is true in robbing the wife of her husband. You operate at the same time and manner as other beasts of prey, in the night season. You say 'Have a good time now and let the morrow care for itself.' You say, 'On with the dance,' no matter at what cost.

"You are the enemy of the home, of chastity, of morality, and of self-mastery in general. You are the enemy of virtue, and of modesty in both men and women, by breaking down the delicate personal reserve that belongs to each sex with reference to the other. That indescribable charm, that dew on the morning rose, that bloom on the butterfly's wing, your touch destroys, so that the better young men about to marry prefer a fresh young woman whose person has not been the property of a lot of chance partners in the dance. You are the enemy of the church and of wholesome amusements at proper hours. You are the enemy of the school by diverting the attention of the pupils and fascinating them with frivolities and unwholesome pastimes.

"You are condemned by the three great tests of business, science, and religion. By business because you are very expensive; you cost far more money and strength than you are worth, and there is a better way to spend the night hours. You are condemned by science, because you are not what you are represented to be; you break the laws of health, and you do not benefit, but injure. You are condemned by religion, because your influence is always away from Christian duties, and toward loose morals, and indifference to sacred things. You do not do right between man and God, nor between man and man. The fact that every shade of Christianity agrees that you would disgrace the church if admitted within its walls proves the real verdict of Christendom to be against you. Any useful act is proper in a church in emergencies. If necessary, a church may serve as a home, school, hospital, or anything harmless, without desecration, but never for a dance. All now agree that it is both silly and disgraceful for gospel ministers and old people to dance; if so, that condemns it for every one. If a thing is wrong in itself for one class, it is wrong for all. Respectable people who admit you, freely acknowledge that you can not be trusted without watching. You lower the standard of morals, and they would not want their friends and young people to follow you to your usual haunts. In short, you are the friend and accomplice of the saloon, the brothel, the gambling den, the white slave trader, the libertine, and of every form of vice.

"These facts will finally be recognized by all persons desiring the highest welfare of humanity. Then you will be forever banished from respectable society, and numerous substitutes, each better than you, will be put where you are now permitted. The only way you can serve me is to give this, my published report of you, the widest circulation possible. You may tell the world that Christian Home knows you too well to give you permission to intrude your fair face, but vile life, into the midst of his young people to their great injury."

THE PRIVATE DANCE.

Many good people commend and practice private dances while they condemn those called public. The fault lies not in the place where the dance occurs, but in the act itself. A rattlesnake in a private garden or public park keeps its own reptile nature, and the same is true of anything good or bad in itself. Persons of means and culture can not, without injury to themselves and others, practice in their exclusive circles and homes any amusement that is bad in a public hall for the dwellers in tenements and lodging houses. The public hall and the unprotected, the unchaperoned, young people simply set the dance free to show its truly bad character. The spirit of progress would make every good thing more accessible to the public. We rightly commend the public schools, libraries, reading-rooms, lectures, churches, museums, art galleries, post-offices, and highways; in short, every good institution can be made public, but that does not include the dance, because it is bad and can only be tolerated under close restrictions. This is proved by the fact that in good society, a dance party of even the most select young people requires the presence of a chaperone.

Wherever the sexes dance together, whether in private or public, it is a perilous offering of fair womanhood to the tiger nature in man. That same nature tamed and held in check, as God meant it should be, contributes to the manliness of man. But when that tiger is indulged, stimulated, and tantalized, it becomes a fierce beast of prey that neither scruples nor halts at any sacrifice, however great to its victim. Its ravages, not only in pagan but also in Christian lands, are terrible. If the better element of the people realized what a struggle the multitude of young and older men have to keep that tiger from doing harm to themselves and others, they would guard the approaches to those dangerous temptations far more carefully. The prices men will pay in money and in loss of character, and the crimes they will commit to still the cravings of that fierce beast in man's nature, ought to convince the whole thinking world that every amusement that tends to arouse its ragings should be banished forever.

The crime of the so-called "art dances" against society is this: They direct the gaze and the thoughts of the men too much toward the figure of the women. These dances have changed neither their nature nor their degrading influence since that fatal day when the daughter of Herodias, by the immodest display of her person, captivated the half-intoxicated Herod and his profligate pagan court. Even that dissolute man was thus led to do what his better judgment condemned. The followers of Herodias in many a wealthy church to-day would officially behead any minister who would preach the whole truth about dancing and those who are to blame for its continuance.

Woman will never be appreciated at her true worth until the gaze and the thoughts of the men are more completely centered on her intellectual, her spiritual, and her higher social nature.

CHAPTER X

THE DEFENSE OF ALCOHOL

SOME very serious complaints have been repeatedly brought against alcohol. It seems fair that any one charged with an offense should be allowed to speak for himself. I have personified alcohol and will let him make his own defense. Mr. Alcohol says:

"I am well aware of the charges made against me. Like much that has been said and written for centuries, these are in the nature of half truths; from one standpoint they are true and from another they are false. In my proper place, I am a great benefit; out of my proper place and wrongly used, I am a great injury. Let me inform you that I am one of the valuable servants of God and man, and that I have a very important office to fill; I must be true to my mission and work, no matter what bad results may follow in some cases. You will be interested in my history from the scientific side.

"My birth came about in this way: You know all plants are composed mainly of a few elements, such as carbon, oxygen, hydrogen, and nitrogen; other elements entering their structure in smaller quantities. A plant is a combination of several of these substances, organized by the principle of life. This organism may be very short-lived and easily broken up, as the mushroom, or it may last through many years like the cedar wood. Now the Creator uses great economy in His management of material. Though He has an immense stock on hand, and could create more, yet He wastes nothing. A plant comes into existence, takes from the earth what material it needs, and organizes it into its own peculiar form and structure. So long as life continues, and for some time afterward, the form of the plant keeps its substance. Sooner or later the principle of decay breaks up the organism and sets that same material free. Certain other forms of life and activity aid in breaking up this organism. A very common agency is the army of insects and worms that devour plants and thus hasten their decay. These dead plants are completely broken up, or rotted, and then the same material becomes food for other plants. One could take a quantity of earth in a box, plant seeds in it, ripen the plants and then let them rot in that box, and produce more plants from the same material to the end of time. In the transit from plant life back to plant food, or rotted material, alcohol is formed. It is formed after decay has carried the plant beyond the limits of food for man and animals, and before it has reached the point of being food for plants. It is one of the steps which lead from the plant back to the soil in which it grows. While the millstones grind the grain and prepare it for food, neither man nor plants can use the millstones for food. While I help prepare plant food, neither man nor plants can use me as a food, for I am poison to both. No animal or man can drink me when I am pure and unmixed; immerse any plant in me and it dies. You see God never intended alcohol as a drink for man any more than He intended that man should eat millstones.

"I am God's servant, and my work is to stand in line with those who grind up the dead plants and prepare food for other plants. I take the material and pass it on to the next one below me. As I reach it to him, man steps in and takes it, and here is where all the trouble begins. When man takes me inside of him, I go right on with my work in his stomach and brain, and through his whole system. I set him crazy, and he does not know or care much what he does. I like my own companions best, so I call for them, and the more I become master of the man the more frequently I

send him after alcohol. I am the same everywhere in wine, .
beer or whisky, though I am mixed with different flavors.

"I am very useful to burn and for various other purposes,
but not to drink—God never meant me for that use. His
Word speaks very plainly against man's abusing me that
way. I am a respectable member of the world's useful
agents. It is only because I have been forced to keep bad
company that I have gotten a bad name. Some men have
discovered that I am a very good trap for catching other
people's money without much work. They do not care
what becomes of the man after they get his money. The
robber kills the man and robs him, then he runs away and
leaves him for others to look after—the liquor dealer does
the same. You must not think I am the servant to such men
as the brewers, distillers, and saloonkeepers; I am their
master and king. I master every man if I get into his system, and I hand him and his property down to the next
one below me. My work is to help feed the plants, and unless they put me in a closed cask, I go on with my work.
If they give me anything to preserve, I keep it until I can
pass it along down on its way to the soil and plant roots.
I am very sorry to harm the innocent women, children and
neighbors, but I am like the hot stove, which, having its
work to do, can not stop because some small child burns his
fingers. He must keep out of the stove's way just as if it
were a railway train. So I must do my work, and man must
learn not to abuse me. A good many blame God for making
me. They might as well blame Him for making fire possible, because they get burned sometimes. Thieves and robbers and men at war burn other people's property a great
many times, but they need not blame God for fire, nor for
alcohol either.

"I am going to make a plea for myself and all of my
friends who are so shamefully abused by bad men. The
friends I refer to are the fruits and the grains that are
spoiled to make bad drinks. Man wastes immense quantities

of grapes, apples, and other fruit, and also vast stores of grain in manufacturing drinks that contain alcohol. The only way to free all of us from such disgrace and abuse is to teach the children better ways. The masses do not yet know the truth concerning alcohol. They do not know my true place, and they begin to drink those liquors of spoiled fruit before they know any better. Teach the children properly; then these children, when grown, will stop finding fault with God for the sins and wrongs that men commit, and they will work with God instead of working against Him."

Alcohol as a beverage is an enormous double loss to the world by turning food into poison, and by the money that is paid out for it. Several per cent of the richest part of the fruit or grain juice is turned into a poison, and consumed with the rest of the liquid. It thus does double work for harm. To skim the cream from milk and throw it away would be wasteful, but to turn it into a poison and leave it in the milk would be a double crime—its presence would neutralize still more of the beneficial ingredients of the milk. That is precisely what is done when grape juice is allowed to spoil, that is, to turn into wine. The sugar becomes alcohol and is not only a loss but is harmful.

It is a sad sight to a thoughtful person to see the poverty in southern Europe, and at the same time know what vast tracts of good land are growing grapes, not to be eaten with all their nourishment, but to have their cream turned into poison, and thus to destroy still more of the food value of that delicious fruit. I had to see the same sin committed in reference to grain in England, Scotland, Ireland and Russia, and in all the other countries to a greater or less degree. Yet all these countries pray God to help the poor. I could not help thinking perhaps He was answering those prayers with the diseases that are destroying the vines in France. As I walked through the vineyards and noticed how the grape vines had been sprayed, I had to think it is better to destroy the vines than to have the wine destroy the people.

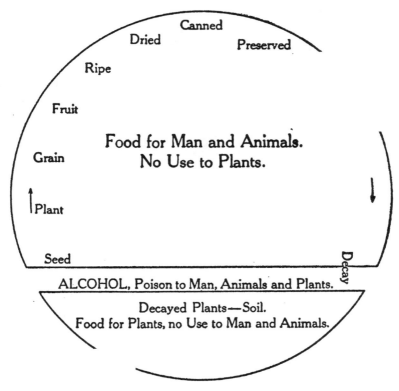

DIAGRAM SHOWING THE PLACE AND PURPOSE OF ALCOHOL.

THE PLACE OF ALCOHOL IN NATURE.

This diagram represents the cycle through which the life of a plant passes it its growth and decay. The seed is planted in the soil, and it grows up into the upper portion, where the plant, the fruit, and the seed are matured which are food for man and animals, but are of no use to other plants. These products can be kept for a time in a dry state, in cans, or preserved; but finally they decay and then they are poison to man and animals, but constitute the food for other plants. On the way down there is a space where alcohol is formed which is poison to man, plants, and animals. Nature does not collect this alcohol in any of her storehouses as she does coal, oil, and minerals, but the space between animal food and plant food illustrates the true scientific place and purpose of alcohol.

The Creator's economy in this process is such that if man will but use his intelligence in avoiding waste and abuse, the same material can pass around the circle, first in the service of man and animals, and then as food for plants, a million times, and alcohol will harm no one, but simply perform its useful part in the series as the Creator intended.

CHAPTER XI

THE CHURCH AND SELF-MASTERY

A CHRISTIAN is one who believes in Christ, and who earnestly strives to imitate His example and to follow His teaching.

A church is an organized body of Christian believers with their officers and ministers.

The work of the church is to lead and assist every individual in the world to master and develop himself after the model, and according to the example and teaching of Jesus Christ.

After several centuries of its existence, a great division in the church began in the following manner: The successive Bishops of Rome sought to make themselves the sole head of the church; to establish themselves as representatives of Christ on earth; and to bring all Christendom under their power and control. Their claims were resisted vigorously, but by grafting the despotic methods of imperial Rome upon the forming life of the new religion, their power grew, and resulted in the division of Christianity. The saddest part of the world's history since the Christian era is connected with this division. There are now practically three great groups, the Roman, Greek, and Protestant churches, but no one of these three branches holds a commanding position of leadership that is recognized by the other two, and by the world in general.

It is time to drop the terms Protestant and Roman Catholic, as these words are very indefinite, and neither term means the same everywhere. One might be the best or worst man on earth, and have his claims as a Protestant or Catholic allowed somewhere. Visit Palestine, Russia, Italy and Mexico, and this fact will be conceded. Let us begin to call the true followers of Christ Christians, no matter what branch of the church they may prefer.

WHAT IS WRONG WITH THE CHURCH?

The great church rulers, instead of elevating the masses, have made their chief aim to subjugate the whole world to themselves. As their first purpose was to ride on the next man's shoulders, and as the next man objected, the most of the ruler's strength was consumed in keeping himself in the saddle, and the other man's strength in getting him off, hence the slow progress of religion. As no father would give to one of several sons a monopoly of any necessity, so that he might rule his brothers; so God would not give to any human being the monopoly of so important a matter as the Christian religion—the only road to the highest manhood and heaven. The claims of Primate of the Church, Vicar of Christ on Earth, or Apostolic Succession, are a species of monopoly which the world rejects.

The church has tried to save the world through the power and agency of religion alone—Christ made no such promise as this for religion. As everything belongs to Him, the agencies of education, religion, business, and science must all be employed in the closest harmony and co-operation for the benefit of man's higher use and nature. Every problem and question in life must be referred to the one of these great departments that can best handle it.

There has been a rivalry among the leaders in these departments, and the church has been the greatest offender in claiming the first place and honors. The Master said, "Whosoever would be the greatest among you, let him be your servant," and "If any man will come after Me, let him deny himself and take up his cross and follow Me." In some churches the higher officials have gone to the other extremes in the luxury and extravagance of their lives, their love of power and preferment, and in resorting to extreme and unjust measures to make themselves both political and religious masters of others.

Other religious bodies have been partly at war with each other; they have been robbing each other, and quibbling over non-essentials in doctrine, to an extent condemned by their own better judgment.

The church has erred in its teaching concerning the sacraments of baptism and the Lord's Supper. There has been strife about the form of administering them, and unreasonable efficacy has been claimed for them; whereas both are rational, scientific, and no more mysterious than the ordinary physical phenomena of our daily lives. The sacraments as Christ used them can be examined from the standpoint of science, religion, experience, or reason, and no sham or weakness can be detected.

Baptism is an initiation service admitting one into the company of Christ's followers. It is a public recognition impressing the mind of the person and the people that such a one has taken this definite step, and implies mutual obligations of helpfulness. It is an outward form in which we follow the example and command of our Lord, using water as a symbol of purity. The age of the person, the amount of water used or the form of applying it, so it be done reverently, are not of vital importance.

When Christ instituted the Lord's Supper, His act was the same as saying, "I give My blood, My life rather than be untrue to My mission of saving the world." When we take the cup we must think, "This represents the blood of Christ in symbol, but our own in reality." That is to say, by this act we commemorate the death of Christ to the extent that like Him we will give up our lives before we will prove false to our promise to follow Him. In symbol, we offer the blood of Christ in sacrifice; in reality, we offer our own, even as He did.

REMEDIES FOR THE CHURCH TO APPLY.

The province of the church is not to master or rule the world, but to lead the world to master itself according to the example and teaching of Christ.

Since no church holds a commanding position of leadership that is recognized by the rest of the world, the leaders of every branch of the universal church must cease to claim any sort of monopoly for their church because of priority, because of numbers, or because of being old or new; and base its right to recognition solely on its actual teaching of the truth. Every church must prove its worth by its fruits, and let others decide on its rank of merit.

The different churches must be honest and observe the Golden Rule with each other. The friendship and good-will of people is as much an item of wealth as money, and it is as surely an act of dishonesty to take one's friends and helpers, as to take one's property. Church members and adherents cost effort and money, and they are of real value to their pastor and the church as surely as sheep or cattle are to their owners. The minister or church that robs a neighbor does a great personal wrong, and also brings dishonor upon the name of Christ. There are those who say, "The man is in error, and I am giving him the Truth." Then give him the truth as a neighborly, Christian act, and tell him to stay among his own people and instruct them. He and his church can then think of you as an honest man, and you will retain their friendship and good-will, and your own self-respect. If your neighbor's sheep were tangled in a wire fence, you would set it free and send it home, you would not claim it as your own. Substitute a sheep for a church member, and you will see the true character and dishonesty of robbing your neighbor church. The world ought to despise the pastor or church that tries to rob a neighbor on any pretext whatever. When ministers and churches become strictly honest with each other regarding their members and friends, much of the strife and friction among them will cease.

Every church must consent to stand in the strongest light and have all its claims, teachings, and methods approved or rejected by the most searching tests for genuineness and utility.

The church must call in the aid of education, science, and business, and employ these agencies to their fullest extent in guarding itself from error and unwise methods, and then it will make far better progress in its great work of saving the world.

A MANHOOD STANDARD NEEDED.

The business world has established a definite standard in coins, weights and measures, which makes possible a vast network of commerce, and the distribution of useful products among the people of the world. There is now an imperative need that the churches should recognize a definite standard and measure of life, conduct, and character. There is no better reason for allowing every person to fix his own standard in religion and character than there is for allowing each one to make his own foot-rule, his own pound-weight, and to stamp his own coins.

Like weights and measures in business, the standard for conduct and character must be one which rises above sex, color, or church preference. Such a standard has been furnished humanity in the life and conduct of Jesus Christ. The boy Jesus was subject to authority; the man, whether workman, teacher, or leader of men, proved His fitness by His courage in Gethsemane and His devotion on Calvary, where He went to His death rather than be false to His trust. The glorified Christ was but the sequence of the obedient boy, the honest workman, and the true man and leader with His courage and fidelity.

The life and conduct of Christ must be recognized as the standard for every age, race, and occupation of mankind. The child can learn to think in units of the Christ life, and to apply this test to himself at the same time he is taught to count his change or to use any standard of measure.

CHURCH ORGANIZATION.

The Church, as an organized body of Christians, can reach its greatest efficiency only through some kind of central intelligence that keeps in vital touch with its several members. Much as a man's head directs the various members of his body in care and service, so the head of the church must keep its energies at work, and see that no portion of the system ceases to do its part, or fails to receive its due. This head, however, is never master, but rather a servant in a high position of responsibility, and must be renewed by the intelligent body of the church as efficiency may require.

The Roman Church has a head, but that head is arbitrary and will not heed the cries of pain in its remoter members. In Mexico, France, and Portugal its feet are suffering, but the head will take no counsel with them; they must obey orders, not suggest methods. This head loves display and loads itself down with crowns and jewels, while it leaves its body to suffer and die for want of attention. This old man gets childish and does not like opposition; he wants to be regarded with extreme veneration, and he even claims infallibility. When the awakened Roman Catholic Church comes to itself, it will drop such a head as that and choose one that is in sympathy with its own body, and will renew this head as need may require.

The English Church claims that John Wesley never left that fold. There was certainly a great change in his church relation and he was driven out to preach in the streets and cemeteries. What did he leave? He took off the grave-clothes of a dead formality and tradition and left them, that was all. If the leaders of the Established Church had done the same, there would have been no Methodist Churches; the need for them would not have arisen. Had the rulers of the English Church followed the example of the commanders of the English navy, and moved forward with the times, that church would have led the world to-day. But no, they still cling to the old sailing ship of Apostolic Succession and the fictitious claim of being the only church. Had the navy done the same, the power of England would be found to-day only in the record of some history and not as a present fact.

Wherein lay the strength of John Wesley's teaching? It was this; he recognized the truth wherever it was found, and accepted it; he recognized the false wherever it might be, and rejected it. He saw the truth in holy living according to the teaching of the Bible, and taught it; he saw the false in the claims and practices of the Established Churches, and repudiated them. If the simple Moravians had the truth, he, a graduate of proud Oxford, would learn from them; if the Bishops and Primates were teaching false doctrines, their authority and dignity had no power to lead him to accept their errors. This is simply what Christ did. He recognized the integrity and honesty of the plain fishermen and chose them as His disciples and representatives; He recognized the falsity of the priests and Pharisees and condemned them for their hypocrisy.

The Methodist Church, the outgrowth of John Wesley's labors, is an organized body bound to a head or central power which is in close touch and sympathy with the remotest part of the church. The selection of this head is in the power of the most vigorous life of the whole church, ministers and laymen. The bishops of the Methodist Episcopal Church are a class of as excellent leaders as the earth affords, but men wear out; therefore when a bishop becomes old he is retired from office, and another man is chosen. Like an efficient army, the church is managed by a vigorous head that is not allowed to become weak through age.

THE CHURCH MUST LEAD THE WORLD.

It is not the province of the church to master the world, because the mastery-of-others is a false system. It is the duty of the church, through its ministers, to lead the world to master itself, after the model and according to the example and teaching of Christ Jesus.

Every person should seek to prepare himself, and aim to inspire his church or society to assume this leadership. As a Christian minister, I call upon my church to lead the world for the following reasons:

The Methodist Church can be examined by the light of the Bible, or science, or experience, or reason concerning all its beliefs, teachings, and methods.

This church is able to replenish its family of ministers and members from its own nursery, and does not need or desire to despoil other churches. It wishes to be a good partner, and has no plan to become the only church, nor to absorb its neighbors. You do not have to leave your church and join ours to get the benefit of our experiences and victories; we believe God is so great that you and I can move in parallel lines toward Him without crowding each other.

This church has a complete organization, which is adapted to all kinds of Christian work, whether religious, missionary, educational, or reform, and it stands ready to exchange any method for a better one on good evidence.

The Methodist Church has dared to place the danger-signal before the doors of these three seductive amusements: the dance, the theater, and gaming-cards, because they face away from the best people and lead in the direction of licentiousness, divorce, and gambling. They are malicious microbes that attack the spiritual life of the young, and cause them to turn away from the field of the ministry, of mission work, and of Christian leadership. Any church that encourages these amusements is liable to find it difficult to supply its pulpits from its own ranks, and may have to seek its ministers elsewhere.

THE CHURCH AND SELF-MASTERY

The world has reached a great crisis in its history. It is time for the church to equip itself for the struggle, step out as a standard-bearer, and summon the leaders of every department of life to follow. The Church must first walk through the fires kindled by genuine religion, true science, and approved experience, and let those fires burn away every defect or error, leaving only that which can stand the test of actual use and benefit to mankind. War, the liquor-traffic, crime, and poverty will speedily be driven from the earth if the churches will only arise in their might, put away all impediments of sin and selfishness, and, clad in the garments of righteousness, follow on in the footsteps of our divine Redeemer.

Christ dedicated to humanity the ministry of three years under the principle of giving up everything, even His life, for the redemption of the world. The pledge was demanded of Him, and He paid it—He died for man and the truth. If the ministers of the Methodist or any other strong church—if one-half of them will dedicate three years of service to the preaching of the whole gospel and the co-operative working of religion, education, business, and science; if they will follow the spirit of the Master's simple life; if they will pledge their fidelity in the communion-cup as He did—they can turn the tide of the thinking world to believe and follow Jesus as the Savior of men. Few, if any, would have to give up their lives. They would not have to sacrifice more than many have done—merely the foolishness, the seductive luxuries, and the superfluous indulgences of the times. Surely many persons will be impressed with the need and the reasonableness of such devotion. Step out and summon your church, your society, your union, or whatever group of persons you may belong to, and appeal for their help in persuading the world to seek and follow its Great Leader.

Oh, my brother men, how small a price to pay for such

a splendid reward—the redemption of the world! The Master offered His life, He paid the pledge, and won the great victory. He knew the prize was worth the cost, and He paid it. Following in His footsteps, and with His example and His divine help, we can turn the thinking world in three years to face about from darkness and begin to march toward the eternal light and freedom.

APPEAL FOR GENERAL LEADERSHIP.

As leaders in the department of religion, our standard shall be the highest development of the individual and the general good of the whole race of men. We call upon the leaders in all lines of human activity to adopt the same standard.

We call upon the men of the legal profession to refuse to employ their services in advancing unworthy men to office or in defending crime, no matter by whom committed; to make the imperative rule in legal proceedings, whether they are engaged for the prosecution or defense, to discover the truth and the facts; to discourage crime and dishonesty, and to defend virtue and the home against all enemies.

We call upon the medical profession to aid in the elimination of disease, and by all scientific and humane methods to protect the present and especially the coming generations. These are in danger from the degeneracy which follows the immoral and vicious habits of parents and other persons in the present customs of society.

We call upon the leaders in science to use their best efforts to elevate humanity by condemning fraud and falsity wherever revealed by their investigations; to seek to eradicate every habit and practice of men that science proves to be prejudicial to the welfare of the young; and to lend their aid and encouragement to the men of other callings who seek to follow the truth and avoid the false and pernicious.

We call upon the teachers and leaders in education to

help in preventing the bad instruction that is given to our children through the evil and destructive habits of older persons; to use their best efforts to place the essentials of education within easier reach of the multitude through simplified spelling and emphasis on the most necessary studies, and to strive to advance the principles of the Great Teacher, who instructed men in the art of being good neighbors and citizens.

We call upon all leaders in business to manufacture and sell only such wares as are beneficial to the general welfare; to cease to furnish intoxicating drinks and harmful drugs to the people, and to oppose and discourage the present waste due to extravagance and the frequent changes in styles of clothing and other articles. In the whole management of business we beg them to place the moral well-being of the people above the gaining of money, the same as teachers and ministers of the gospel are now expected to do; to feel that the business man has as great a responsibility for the welfare of the community as the Christian minister, and to consider that he has no more right to encourage vice and immorality by his wares than the minister has by his life and teaching.

CHAPTER XII

THE BIBLE AND SELF-MASTERY

THE Bible is a collection of books giving the best knowledge and wisdom of all antiquity touching man's duty to God and his fellow-man. It is the great liberator and educator of mankind, and therefore every nation should encourage all its citizens to study and obey its precepts. It is not more bullets that the world needs, but more Bibles.

A belief in the Bible makes a man more intelligent; it teaches him the facts about human nature, and consequently about himself.

It makes a man free by teaching him the truth, and thus keeping him from the bondage of error and ignorance.

It makes a man honest by showing him that whatsoever a man soweth, that shall he also reap. If he sows dishonestly, he will reap dishonesty.

It makes a man master of himself; then he does not allow himself to harm others, nor does he allow others to harm him.

"By their fruits ye shall know them" applies to the Bible, and it is according to the principles of science and of the Bible itself to measure any force by the work it has accomplished. I refer to the following historic facts to prove the value of the Bible in making men intelligent, upright, and free.

THE BIBLE IN ENGLAND AND SPAIN.

Years ago there was a time when Spain had more territory than England. The power of England, representing at that time the British Empire of to-day, was afraid of Spain, and with good reason. Had not a storm destroyed the Spanish Armada, the course of history would probably have been very different. We can not place any blame upon the Spanish people, nor can we give any credit to the English people for the part that was played by the rough sea in deciding the victory. The history of Spanish navigators and explorers in that early time proves them to have been able, courageous men. Spanish masters of the sea and of arms discovered and took possession of the new world in advance of the English.

Again, the traveler in Spain to-day who makes himself acquainted with the average type of the Spanish people as they are engaged in the necessary work of life must acknowledge that they have the qualities of faithful, efficient men and women—the Spanish people are made of good material. I have traveled somewhat extensively in Spanish lands, and also in British countries. The quality and fiber of both these peoples, from the earliest times to the present, are excellent. It is not the question which excels. History would make it difficult to prove either better or worse than the other. In the earlier years Spain had the advantage part of the time. To-day Spain has lost all her colonies, while England has kept hers, or she has the close friendship of them all. We in America know well that it is British civilization and the freedom and intelligence which that civilization brings with it that has made us a great nation, and we gladly acknowledge the source of our benefits. The people of America and England know that a strife or war between them could not result in gain to either, but in great loss to both.

What has made the difference between Spain and England? It is not that the English people are better than the Spanish. The difference between Spain and England which has come about in the last few centuries lies in this fact: the powers which ruled in Spain burned the Bible and kept it from the common people; the powers which ruled in England published the Bible, wove its truth into the national life, and encouraged its use among the people.

To-day, wherever British civilization has gone and taken the Bible with it, we find intelligence, prosperity, and freedom. We find stability of government, we find safe investments in property, and we find a large measure of justice rendered to all.

Compare the people and lands where Spanish civilization has gone and holds the balance of power. We find the Bible is still forbidden and is still burned. Where it is sold, except by missionaries and agents from other countries, it is expensive and hard to find. I have hunted for it personally in these lands, and speak from first knowledge. There is a great lack of intelligence, prosperity, and freedom. Property investments are not safe, and there is a measure of injustice on every side. Honest toil is regarded with disfavor, while idleness and luxury are looked upon as the marks of excellence; hence the advance of the chief lines of industry is led by foreigners. The governments are very unstable. It is easy for the one who is defeated in an election to gather a sufficient force of men into bands either to overthrow the government or to keep the country in turmoil and bloodshed much of the time.

Why is this possible? For two reasons: some of the leaders are devoid of principle, and many of the people are so ignorant and wretched that a few glowing promises will easily lead them to plunder and kill their own countrymen in hope of something better.

Several hundred years ago these two branches of the human race were essentially equal; to-day they are very unequal. The change has not come about by virtue of the superiority of the English people as such over the Spanish, but by the elevating power and influence of the Bible which was woven into the life of the English people but forcibly withheld from the Spanish people. No other explanation will suffice to account for the divergence between these two nations, once so nearly equal but now so different.

Permit me to copy a few reflections and convictions that

were impressed upon me in Madrid a few days after my sixtieth birthday. I had been seriously reviewing my own past life and the history of the human race

"I do not understand all of mathematics. I have spent much time and labor upon the subject, but its mysteries are still beyond me; yet I know enough of the rudiments to keep my own accounts with the world in business and count my change. Those who are in a position of power and wealth owe it to every child of the world to teach each one to read and write, and enough of arithmetic to count his change and keep his accounts with his neighbors in business.

"I do not understand all of the Bible and God's system for guiding men through life and eternity, but I do understand enough to keep my accounts with God, with myself, and with my fellow-men. I know the Golden Rule and its application. Those in power and wealth owe it to all the children of the earth to teach them enough about the Bible and God to enable them to keep their own accounts with Him, with themselves, and with their fellow-men. The child must be taught to care for his money among strangers; likewise he must be taught to take care of his character among strangers."

WHAT IS WRONG WITH THE BIBLE?

To the question, What is wrong with the Bible? it could truthfully reply, "I have been wounded in the house of my friends, and, thus disabled, I have been prevented from doing my full work." Men have not been fair with the Bible. Different leaders have tried to marshal all the friends and forces of humanity in their following by some forced interpretation that seemed to serve their purpose. The great aim and use of the Bible is to place in the hands of each person the intelligence, the freedom, and the honesty necessary to make him a follower of God and true to his fellowmen. Its aim is not to make certain men masters of others, but to make each one a master of himself. If you and I follow God, we shall move in parallel lines, we shall have plenty of room, and we shall not hinder, but instead we shall help each other. If either of us attempts to ride on the shoulders of the other, or to compel the other to take orders from him and follow in his footsteps, there will be trouble. The influence of the Bible is to make us friends, walking side by side. Without it, each of us may easily leave his own path, trespass on the other, and get into strife and conflict. That is the world's history in too large a measure in all the past. The Bible can change that bad method for a good one.

HOW SHALL WE APPROACH THE BIBLE?

We ought to approach the Bible as men approach a gold-mine. They go to get gold and any other metal that is of value. There is always earth and rock in the way, and it is closely mixed with the gold. This coarser material does not deter them. They move it aside, take as much gold as they can secure, and make it their own. They go very far to get it, and suffer all kinds of privation. They are determined to find treasure if possible.

How do many act when coming to the Bible? They see what appears to be earth and coarse material, and they begin by examining these. They report that the gold has earth mixed with it; it is not already in bars or stamped coin. They try to measure how much earth there may be in the mixture. Different critics compare notes, and they seem to claim honor and distinction in proportion to the amount of coarse material they find—not how much gold to the ton, but how much earth. Thus, the less gold, the greater the find, because with little gold there is more room for earthy material.

The gold in the mines is the pure gold, but it is scattered among the common rocks and earth in a natural way. The gold of the Bible is the real truth, but it is scattered along the centuries in the lives of actual human beings like ourselves. The Bible tells us in a few brief paragraphs something of the beginning of things and of man. Then it recounts something of God's revelation of truth and the great facts that man needed to know. Mingled with these it records notable failures of persons who disobeyed God, and notable benefits that came to those that followed Him and obeyed Him. It is a very natural class of people the Bible mentions; it commends only the good, it condemns only the bad. It shows marvelous patience on the part of God in His dealings with men, even the bad ones. He who goes to the Bible for gold will find gold, and more than he can carry away. He can send his friends to the same mine; it is too rich and large for monopoly.

I can not understand how any one who wishes to do his full part in the world and take no more than his share, can refuse himself the help of the Bible in so great a task. I do not see how any one who is desirous of elevating humanity, of making every human being intelligent, honest, and free, and of extending the blessings of peace and prosperity over the earth, can neglect so great an agency for good in his noble undertaking.

CHAPTER XIII

LABOR AND SELF-MASTERY

A WAR between labor and capital is irrational and suicidal. Capital is the result of man's labor applied to the resources and products which God has stored in the earth for man's use. A strife between labor and capital is therefore a quarrel between man and what he has produced. One class of men is not born and fated to remain capitalists, and another to remain laborers. Each was created to be first laborer, and then capitalist in some degree. A house divided against itself can not stand. It falls, and both builder and owner must share the loss in the end, because something has been destroyed. Something has been lost, and that loss must be borne by some one. This is best illustrated when the builder and the owner is the same man. When they are two different men, the owner will raise the rent to provide for such loss. The laborer is therefore robbing himself when he causes the destruction of property in a strike.

The capital-and-labor problem is all a question between man and man. It is the minds of the men on both sides that must be changed. Change places as they are now; put labor-leaders and agitators in the places of the capitalists; let them own and control the same millions, and let the present capitalists turn laborers, or simply disappear, and it is a question whether conditions would not become worse. The new masters might be more tyrannical than the old, and the new workmen would still be banded against them.

Let this be done: Change the minds of the men on both sides; make all intelligent on the true principles of labor and capital; make each honest in his particular sphere, and trouble and friction will disappear. One of two results would have to follow: either the two parties, as now constituted, would become fair and just toward each other, or the laborers, being in the vast majority in numbers, would cease to waste their energies and earnings on liquor, tobacco, and expensive living. They would learn to use money more wisely, and would soon have capital and ability to build factories and control the situation entirely.

WAR-METHODS CAN NOT FORCE THE EARTH.

No strikes or lockouts could ever compel an acre of ground to increase its production of grain by one single ounce; that must be done by following more closely the laws of the soil and plant-growth. Likewise any increase in business investment must be caused by an improvement in the conditions favorable to such increase. The desired change absolutely refuses to come through war-methods, such as strikes, boycotts, and lockouts. These methods may shift some temporary advantage to one side or the other for a time, but with loss to both capitalists and laborers, or to the still larger party, the public, who buy the products. War-methods are always at the advantage of the few who are in command, either by chance or fraud, or by that genius for getting money which is possessed by only a few, like the genius for art, music, or any other special talent. The methods of peace and the principles of justice founded on intelligence, honesty, and self-mastery are the only methods that give the multitude a fair chance. War-methods have been tried for thousands of years as a means of settling disputes between man and man, and have failed utterly. The improvements that have come in connection with those methods have been in spite of war, and not because of it. War-methods count in favor of the few against the many. The many get in each other's way, and while they are righting themselves, the few in power, old ones or new ones, carry off the booty. The monkey will still eat the cheese over which the cats in the fable quarreled, and he is the only one to gain by the dispute.

Let us illustrate the case. Place one thousand suits of clothes in a row, in separate bundles two feet apart. Make the chances as fair as possible; place one thousand men in a line at some distance from the clothes, and at a given signal let them rush and get what they can. The result may be easily imagined: there will be many sore heads and torn clothes. This is labor and capital at war in a strike. Now put one thousand suits of clothes in a store. Tell one thousand men to go and work, earn money, save it, and buy the clothes—the first money gets the first suit. Compare results. There will be no waste, no new clothes ruined, no capital destroyed, no bad spirit, and no grudges remaining between man and man. The greatest gain would be the mastery of self and resources, in place of mastering others. The world must be redeemed through the mastery of self and soil, not through the conquering of others and compelling them to pay tribute into our hands.

A WORD TO THE FEW AND A WORD TO THE MULTITUDE.

There is a very strong tendency on the part of those in command in the great corporations of property on the one hand, and of the great labor combinations on the other, to issue arbitrary orders concerning the prices and the sale of commodities, and also regarding the prices and hours of labor, with ruinous restrictions for any independent spirit that will not bow to those in authority. It will help very little if the world is simply to change masters and still be ruled by despotism. It is impossible to fix arbitrarily the prices and hours of labor or the income for investments. It is imperative to have honest wares, honest labor, and honest prices for both, and then reasonable conditions for those concerned with labor or with capital. After this, each must be left free to work little or much, as his strength will allow, and to receive pay accordingly. If some persons wish simple clothing, plain barbering,. and other service for a moderate price, and others desire a more expensive service, reason and common sense would decide that both ought to be accommodated, and we should not permit laws that compel the less competent to stop work and be supported by the public, nor should we place the required skill and the prices for service out of the reach of a large number of people. No one has the right to live by fraud or plunder, but within the range of right and justice it is necessary to allow very large freedom to suit the needs of the great variety of persons, tastes, and conditions of men. If one man wants a fifteen-cent lunch and another wants a thirty-cent lunch, how absurd it would be to pass a law that any restaurant should furnish only the one class or the other. But this would be as reasonable as it is to fix by law the price of any commodity or service. Make men intelligent and honest, and then set them free, is absolutely the only principle that can be worked in this world without intolerable despotism and injustice.

The ancient empires were little more than great systems of spoliation of the many by the few, who, with the power of the sword in the hand of despotism, enslaved and robbed the multitude while they themselves lived in barbaric luxury and insane extravagance. The tendency to-day is to reverse this, and the multitude is inclined to despoil the few rich men by means of taxation through the power of the ballot, and to live on short labor-days, great damages for accidents, and pensions. When the many know their power, they can always outvote the few, and now they are tempted to vote pensions for the aged, the widows, and the orphans, and for all who are disabled by accident or disease. They assume that the rich men and the corporations can pay all the cost.

Both systems are bad—the few despoiling the many with the sword, or the many despoiling the few by the ballot and taxation. The only hope of the world is through the intelligence and honesty of the few and also of the many, so that each will earnestly strive to support himself, and not try to rob his neighbor, or even seek to live at the expense of others. Intelligence to know the true principles of life, combined with the honesty and courage to live by those principles, is the only safe rule and also the one hope of this awakening world of humanity. The world at large can accept no smaller aim than the determination to make the last man intelligent and honest, so that he can be trusted with the power of his one ballot or with the power of any office, from the lowest to the highest, whether of the government, or some labor union, or great business corporation.

AN APPEAL TO OTHER TOILERS.

All you who toil in useful labor with hand and brain the world around, to you I appeal. Born and bred to toil myself, and having searched the world for knowledge, to you I bring my treasures. To you I fling open the only door to prosperity that is wide enough for all the world to pass through—the only door that admits all to regions of enduring prosperity and happiness. I have called it the self-mastery system. To pass through this door you need drop only the vices which rob you and your children of your money and your manhood; drop those that deceive you with false promises of pleasure and satisfaction at the very time they are binding chains of servitude upon you. While they soothe your brain into inaction, they place chains of perpetual servitude upon your feet.

Take as your liberator and model the Hero of Calvary; He was a toiler, and He won the great victory. He conquered self and the world's resources and products, and He did it to mark out the way for us. He mastered not only life and the world, but even death itself. By following Him you and I can do the same. By the use of the knowledge and the powers He has placed within our reach we can stave off the grim boatman until our time comes, not his. We can make him wait until, ripe with years and service, we shall say to him: "Come now; I am ready to cross the river called Death; I need your aid. I thank God that through His divine assistance you have become my servant, and not my master."

It lies within our power to give to every child a noble birth, and to aid him to build a mastered manhood that will walk through life, and step into eternity a crowned victor.

CHAPTER XIV

THE NATION AND CRIME

CRIME is so far-reaching in its character that every criminal act goes beyond the one convicted, and implicates others; and it is certain that no person goes to prison being the only one to blame. The sooner we recognize this fact, and the sooner each one looks himself over thoroughly to find what portion of blame rests on himself, the better for all. The next problem is to analyze the case and apply an appropriate remedy.

The world says to ministers of the gospel and to teachers, "You must be upright; you must do right between man and man; you are allowed no latitude." It says to the politicians, "You ought to be upright, but we do not require it." It says to the lawyers, "We do not really expect you to be honest." A lawyer may use any or all tricks picked up by his craft to defeat justice. The State may spend thousands of dollars to capture a criminal, and then one or more shrewd lawyers can be hired to use any means known to free him. They pick the jury with that end in view; they intimidate witnesses; they resort to all possible technicalities; they bluster and try to confuse the counsel for the State; in short, they too often disregard the rights of the honest public in their zeal to defend a criminal. They do all this for the mere hire of money and fame, working directly against the people and the State; and some get rich at it. There is no more reason why one set of men should turn against the honest people by defending criminals than there is for teaching crime to the children as an honorable vocation. This comes from a pernicious tradition which has assumed that the law is a thing by itself, and is to be upheld and defended at all costs and in defiance of justice to the people. Religion is not the only field that is cursed by bad tradition. Criminal law-practice is pernicious; it is known to be so; but because many talented men get both wealth and fame by it, crime is encouraged, and little progress for the better is made.

WHAT IS WRONG IN THE MANAGEMENT OF CRIME?

The penalty has been centralized too much upon the one who was caught and who lacked money or influence to defend him, and too little attention has been paid to the persons and conditions that made him a criminal.

Crime has been allowed to become profitable; first, to those who actually commit the crime—the primary criminals; and second, to those who help them escape punishment —the secondary criminals.

It has been allowed to become respectable and profitable for professional men to appear in open court and secure a verdict which pronounces criminals innocent and sets them free.

In the name of justice to all concerned, it is impossible to see why the aim of both sides of the case should not be *to find out the truth in the matter and stop the crime.*

The nation, in its capacity as an individual, owes it to itself not to allow one of its members to fatten by devouring another member. There are those who claim that the criminal is in many cases defective in intellect, and not wholly responsible; then he should not be set free until he can be trusted. Criminals who commit stupid crimes may be adjudged to be stupid; those who commit skillful crimes must be admitted to have intelligence that makes them responsible. It is no kindness to the professional criminal to encourage him to continue in his vicious ways.

One way in which secondary criminals make money is this: A fraudulent company is formed to exploit a mine, a land-improvement enterprise, or other business venture. In this case the persons forming the company are the primary criminals. Their agents who sell fraudulent securities, and the banks that buy fraudulent notes against good property, are the secondary criminals who greatly profit by the crimes of the first. They should be made responsible for their conduct and their part in the wrong to the community. We have a parallel in another line of business. The grocer and the druggist are not allowed to sell any substance unless they know what it is, and if it is of a dangerous character, it must be so labeled. A prison sentence for agents who sell fraudulent mining and other stock, and for bankers and others who buy fraudulent notes secured against unwary people, would make those men more cautious and far more honest. This would protect many teachers, clerks, farmers, and other busy people desirous of investing their earnings, and yet not acquainted with the tricks of smooth-tongued sharpers.

TO DISCOURAGE CRIME.

Place the lawyers, both for the prosecution and defense, under oath that they will neither strive to free a guilty person nor to convict an innocent one; that their sole aim shall be to find the truth in the case, to free the innocent and to punish the guilty. If the persons accused of crime felt that the aim of the attorneys on both sides was to free them if innocent, and to convict them if guilty, crime as a profession would very soon cease. Make it a misdemeanor for a lawyer to try to defeat justice the same as it is for a witness to perjure himself. Make it neither profitable nor respectable to help set criminals free to continue in acts of crime.

Arouse public sentiment to the necessity of having one definite standard of conduct and manhood for ministers, teachers, lawyers, politicians, and all other classes of people. If lawyers will follow the honesty of Abraham Lincoln and refuse to defend those whom they have good reason to believe or know are guilty, and if they will cease to hire themselves out to become the attorneys of liquor men and others whose business injures and corrupts humanity, very rarely would any intelligent person definitely plan to commit a crime. The crimes committed on a sudden impulse and by irresponsible persons could be easily prevented or cared for. If the lawyers would boycott criminals and criminal practice, the number of crimes would diminish amazingly, and with vast gain to every State and every citizen of this world.

Should any person think me too severe against certain practices of the lawyers, let me remind him that I have the whole legal profession back of me as a precedent. The lawyer by his own creed and practice assumes that his client is innocent and that his cause is just; then he proceeds to win his case against all odds. I am sure that my client—the childhood of the world—is innocent, and that this cause is a righteous one. It is therefore not only my right, but also my duty to defend my clients, the children, against wrong and injustice from all sources.

The liquor-traffic could be made to cease by allowing no new recruits to its ranks, and by requiring the business to stop with the death of those who are now engaged in it and who make a living by it, and thus no one would be thrown out of employment. Likewise that portion of legal practice which now lives by defending crime and criminal business could be stopped by permitting no new recruits to this part of the profession, and letting it die with those who now live by carrying it on.

DIVORCE.

For divorce cases establish a tribunal, paid by the State, and allow no one to make money by the profession of separating husband and wife, as is now done by divorce lawyers.

Let the intelligent people candidly and earnestly seek to learn what customs in society tend toward the separation of husbands and wives, and let this same intelligence honestly and courageously apply the necessary remedies, and the first dangerous steps in the direction of divorce will be avoided in a multitude of cases. The interview between Mr. Christian Home and Mr. Dance given in the chapter on "Amusements" touches some vital points in the causes of divorce.

THE NATION AND POVERTY.

We often hear the remark that "it is no disgrace to be poor." That depends on the cause of the poverty. If one is poor because he was honest and would not take advantage of others, because he had to support dependent relatives, or for any good and sufficient reason, it is no disgrace. Poverty is a disability, and it keeps one from privileges which he needs and should have. If a man has been idle, or drunken, or wasteful, and poverty has come to him by his own fault, he is disgraced by it. Back of him stand those who taught him bad habits or failed to teach him better ones. The merchants who crowded wares on him that he could not afford, whether it was strawberries in March or other extravagances in living, helped him down. Those who paraded fine clothes before him and made him ashamed of his plainer ones, helped to keep him poor. The truth is, we are our brother's keeper, and we are all bound together in a network of common interest. There is needed a greater sympathy for the weak or unfortunate members of society, and a necessity of better methods being applied to improve them. It is important to study the causes of extreme poverty and of immense wealth more thoroughly than we have done, and thus be able to adjust these matters better.

There is nothing to be said against praying for the poor, unless it means that we thus try to shift our responsibility upon God. It might be better to pray for ourselves, that we may have intelligence and frugality, and that we may set a Christian example that would do away with poverty.

The life of Jesus furnishes us a sure model, if we will but use it.

The liquor-traffic, war, tobacco, and gambling are great causes of poverty which we have no excuse for continuing and carrying into the next generation. Those who hold the power of wealth, charge higher prices, take larger profits, and pay less for services than is just, in order to feed their craving for display and their love for personal indulgence.

The pernicious tradition from paganism, that it is respectable to be idle and live on the earnings of others, either relatives or the public, is an important cause of crime and poverty.

PENSIONS AND SELF-MASTERY.

The pension system is unsound in principle and tends to dependency and weakness. It loads down any business such as a bank, factory, railway, or the State with the debts of one generation for the next to pay. It will hamper the old firm with a load of pensioners, in competition with a new one yet free from such burdens. It is uncertain for the pensioners, as the business may fail to earn enough to live and pay the salaries of its present force and also a list of past employees.

It encourages improvidence and the spending of all one's income, because one is looking to get a pension to support him later.

The only true business principle is for each one to cut down expenses, and thus increase his income and save money to pension himself. This makes each one independent, enforces economy, discourages waste and extravagance, and protects the business and the public treasury from increasing burdens.

WE CAN NOT LEAVE THIS WORK TO THE FEW.

In every class the few persons in command, whether because of money or of influence, are intoxicated with the love of their own personal luxuries and their power over others. Their spirits are poisoned with the venom of their own selfishness. We, the people, have waited long enough for those at the top to reach down and help us up. We shall wait in vain for such help, for they are chiefly engaged in holding their places on other men's shoulders by taking advantage of the ignorance and incompetence of the masses. God meant that a bird should rise by cultivating the powers that He has built into the very constitution of the bird's nature, and by which he is master of the elements. God meant that the masses of humanity should rise by developing the powers that He has built into the very constitution of each individual. Let the birds in the human nest cease to chirp and beg the larger ones to carry them on their backs by means of sick-benefits, alms-houses, and old-age pensions. These may be needed for a short time during the transition to better ways, but they are only temporary— they are only pontoon-bridges for emergencies. We must study the Master's ways and methods, and each will then learn to do all these things for himself. Let us cease trying to master our employers; we shall never get what we wish in that way. We must begin by mastering ourselves, and then strive to lead every individual to win by this same true principle. With the example and help of the Man of Galilee, the Hero of Calvary, who labored with mind, heart, and hand, we can conquer and lead the whole world to certain and enduring victory.

CHAPTER XV

WAR AND SELF-MASTERY

THE principles of war and the qualities necessary for its prosecution, such as strength, courage, obedience to commands, and self-sacrifice, were never intended to be employed by one man in gaining the mastery over another. Man needs all his strength, courage, self-denial, and other virtues to aid him in subduing and developing the earth and to make him sure of mastering his own powers for good. War is an intensely sad perversion of these qualities in an effort by the few to rule the rest of the world.

Man was created with so much of the divine possibilities of will-power, talent, and energy that he must struggle valiantly first to understand the plan of his being, and then to gain the wise mastery of this same wonderful being. Man must be created intelligent; he must have hands and feet for his use, and he must have an independent will-power. The great final contest is for him to master this whole bundle of talents and powers, and to make it self-governing among other beings younger and weaker than himself. It would be impossible and absurd to have a policeman over each person; it is entirely possible and practical to produce and train a race, every individual of which shall be his own policeman and guardian. The final aim is that all shall be intelligent, all strong and capable, all honest and trustworthy, and, by virtue of these powers, all entirely free. All must be self-masters, self-servants, and mutually helpful wherever help is needed.

The principle of war is a contest between two or more persons to gain some advantage by force or violence. This conflict occurs between two individuals, or units. The possible contestants may be two persons, two families, two tribes or clans, or two nations.

IS WAR INEVITABLE?

War is not necessary; it can be stopped forever. A vast number of instances in all civilized countries in which two families or two cities have lived together in entire harmony, proves this possibility. As we reach the units composed of a larger number of persons, such as States, provinces, and nations, we find the difficulties increase, and war becomes more probable from the fact of there being fewer personal acquaintances, and also a greater number of avenues through which trouble may enter and break the peace.

Let us approach this problem from the point where actual war is going on. Picture for yourself any war you choose, and let us ask some questions of the combatants. We will go directly to the battlefield. Here are two men on opposing sides, trying to kill each other. We say to the first one, "Has that man you are fighting harmed you in any way?"

"No, sir; I never saw him before; I do not know his name; I can not speak his language."

We ask the man on the other side the same question, and receive the same answer. Then we ask, "Why are you fighting that man?"

The answer is, "I was ordered to do so by my officer." The other man gives the same reply.

We go to the officer who ordered those men and their comrades to begin battle, and ask him, "Why did you give your men the order to attack those yonder?"

He replies, "I simply obeyed the commands given me to deliver, and ordered the fight." The officer on the other side gives the same answer. Either side may say they were defending themselves from attack, but this fact changes nothing in principle. The privates and minor officers simply obey the orders of the higher officers in either case.

We pursue this course until we reach the commanding general. He says the emperor, the king, or the president issued a declaration of war; or that the other nation declared war, and we are defending ourselves. In a large number of cases the cause of war can be traced to two persons, or even to one. At times the cause was two families who quarreled for property, or, as in wars of succession, it was for the crown.

Let us view the field from another point. We will go again to the common soldier and ask him, "Have you anything against that man on the other side?"

"No; I do not know him."

"Very well; stop fighting!" giving the same order to both sides. Now we go to the officers of each army and say, "Tell your superiors those men find they have no quarrel, and they refuse to fight." Finally we reach the one who declared war.

"Sire, the men and officers say they have no disagreement with each other, and they have ceased fighting. They say, if you have any quarrel with that king or general, you and he must fight it out between yourselves, and that there is neither reason nor justice in so many persons slaughtering one another without cause. Sire, why do you not fight your own battles?"

Let the facts of history answer this question.

"I wanted more glory; I wanted more territory; I wanted more power and luxury; I wanted to rule that nation; I wanted to ride on the shoulders of other people; I did not want to earn my own living, nor to pay for it: I preferred to get it by robbery and violence."

The usual cause for war is the desire of one or more persons to get more than their share, to get what belongs to others, without earning it, and the fault always rests on the leaders or those in power. They say the people did so and so, but the beginning and end of every war is pronounced by the authority of a very few persons.

WHO IS TO BLAME FOR WAR?

The leaders, whether emperors, kings, nobles, or generals. They are dishonest, and begin war by their own unjust conduct. They do far less than their part, and take enormously more than their share. Many of the warriors of the past have had the heart of a wolf and the courage of a rabbit. Animals fight their own battles. Often the kings and other rulers keep in the background during the fight, but spring to the front with great gusto when the triumphal procession is to take place.

The chief one in authority is to blame. Next comes his highest official, who carries out a barbaric order for war. If he were not an arrant coward or thoroughly bad at heart, he would refuse to issue such an order. A good, respectable dog will not bite little pigs. When sent to drive them out, he will run over them and frighten them, but will not tear their tender flesh. History gives many instances where the king's dog, his cringing officer, has not spared women, children, or any one that seemed to stand in the way of his master's selfishness, lust, or greed. The one to suffer may even be at times the ruler's own father, mother, son, daughter, or any other relative. The number of persons who suffer and the extent of their sacrifice and loss has little effect on the ruler who has the power to push them between himself and danger. Such a ruler will not yield until in personal peril of either bodily hurt or loss of power or territory. When these are in real danger, he is ready to treat for peace.

WHO GAINS BY WAR?

In the larger sense, no one gains. There is a loss to both sides, because war always means bad feeling, frightful waste, lingering suffering, destruction, and death. The leaders on the winning side claim great honor and glory for their deeds of carnage. If any act when performed by two persons is not justifiable, to increase the number by two hundred or two hundred thousand only magnifies the wrong.

There is neither glory nor honor in slaying one's fellow-men; that is one of the falsehoods of tradition. The boasted glories of war rest solely on the perfidy of pagan tradition. We ought to fling tradition into the crucible and kindle the fire of truth beneath it hot enough to burn away the corruption and false teaching that the savagery of our ancestors has left to hinder human progress.

REMEDIES FOR WAR.

Cease to make warriors of the children. Cease to teach them that a warrior is thereby a hero and to be honored; teach them the true nature and causes of war, and prepare them to settle their disputes by reasonable methods.

The army and navy officers are ever clamoring for more expensive armaments. Stop paying big pensions to these officers when retired; they can economize and pension themselves as well as millions of other persons whose income is less than the pay these officers receive.

Stop building monuments for great battles and for war heroes; it is hard enough to forgive and forget injuries without being reminded of them by costly records in bronze and marble. Both sides of an unjust war build monuments, and thus teach their children to hate each other, and to seek an occasion for revenge. If the dead have merits, let them be honored in ways that will not perpetuate the conditions which made their sacrifices necessary.

THE SPIRIT OF THE WARRIOR.

The spirit of the true warrior and hero—the obedience to commands, the devotion to an aim, the indifference to personal comfort and suffering, and the readiness to sacrifice anything or everything for others, all of which are trained into the life of the soldier—is sorely needed to-day. This spirit is needed not in slaying our fellow-men, not in going to death for some selfish leader, nor in compelling men to combine in the interests of church, party, labor, capital, or any other narrowing impulse. Heroic men and women are needed in attacking the abuses of the times and the vices of the politicians and of society. The enemies of man to be assailed by the spirit of the true warrior are the practice of war itself, the liquor-traffic, the slavery of tobacco and other harmful drugs, the tyranny of fashion in clothing and other necessities, the despotism of both capitalists and laborers, wastefulness of natural resources, graft, crime, and the general spirit of selfishness and oppression. We need to fight the frauds and shams in religion, in law, in medicine, in business, and in society; in a word, we need to strive against everything that hinders the progress of humanity.

If all were to join in this battle, it would cause real sacrifice to none, it would be a gain for each and every one, and the victory would be easily won. A vast multitude of good people would have to give up only some foolishness or even harmful indulgence to secure priceless benefits to the millions of the coming generations. Alas! those who are comfortable in the old ruts are fixed in their preferences, and do not wish to change. Appeal to them, and they tell you all is well, and they are satisfied with things as they are. Those in power hold the uncomfortable classes so firmly that they can not change if they would; the hands and feet of many are tied by circumstances, and some comfortable person holds the cords and will not relax his grip. It remains then a task of true heroism for those persons who care for the world's advancement to adopt the type of the soldier's simplicity of life and his indifference to personal gain, and fight against the wrong instead of fighting men, until the great world-victory is won for enduring peace and universal justice.

CHAPTER XVI

A WORLD-VISION AND SELF-MASTERY

THE acorn can begin its life with a handful of moist earth in a little earthen pot. Erelong such small quarters will stop the growth of the plant; more room is needed. For the full development of the oak, it must have abundant room for its roots in the soil and its branches in the air. How much space does an oak require? Enough to allow both roots and branches to keep on growing without reaching any barrier. Man's bodily growth very easily finds room, and does not require much space; the mind, the spirit, needs more. I believe it needs this whole earth, and the universe about it. The present need is for each individual to have some idea and vision of the whole human race as the boundaries of the space his hope and faith are to occupy. Each member of the family needs a vision reaching to every member of the family; each member of the nation needs a vision as large as his nation; each member of the world's population needs a vision as large as the world. Is this too much to ask? Surely not of the world's leaders; and to such this appeal is addressed. I know no better way of mastering self than to get a clear vision of the greatness and importance of the rest of the world. I am small compared with the world, but I am great in my power to grasp it somewhat and help it along. If I work hard, if I get little pay, if I spend little money on myself and more on others, if I do anything that goes beyond my own realm of personal needs, I see that it pays, that it is worth while.

This chapter, like others of this book, will be in some sense a diary of ideas as they came to me in travel, because of having a world-vision and still seeking a larger one. The vision I have of the great mass of the busy people who are doing the necessary work of the world is that they are worthy. They are doing well, and deserve a better chance than they have had. Spain was a new country to me, and seemed farther away than some other parts of Europe. It was, however, my joy to look out of the car-window and think of the common worker as my friend who helped make that journey possible and pleasant. So I wrote in my notes thus: "I am thankful to the capitalists, the engineers, the common workmen, and all who had any part in building this railroad. The same is true on ship-board, and also of any conveniences and privileges which I use. I eat fruit and other food from remote parts of the earth. I am thankful to all those who help in this line, including those who raise and transport bananas, figs, rice, or any other useful articles." It was my joy to see these people and live among them as friends and neighbors. I tried to feel with them, and think with them, and now I can not think lightly of them. I can grow enthusiastic over the common people of every land I have seen. Plenty of faults, of course, they have, but the blame lies not so much on them as on those who eat the fruits of their poorly-paid labor and do nothing to enlighten and elevate them to the place they ought to occupy. Was I above them in intelligence and power? Usually I was; and why? Because of better opportunities. If I help them up, will it help or hurt me? It will help me to all I hold most important. I greatly prefer good neighbors, with the thought that my neighborhood meets itself, starting where I live and traveling both ways around the earth. If I could know that within a reasonable time all the children of the world would have as fair a chance in life as I have had, it would be the best I could wish for them. Not that this would mean perfection, but it would mean that they could go on and improve matters as rapidly as they chose.

I never have entered any door of opportunity that I

would not gladly leave wide open behind me, that all might enter. To leave such doors unlocked is my aim in spending so little on my food, clothing, and personal indulgences. To me it is not sacrifice, but an investment of a permanent nature; it is an annuity not for life only, but for eternity. The difference between the price of first and third-class steamer-fares is to me a contribution to world-improvement. I believe I am making a better investment than the man who rides first-class. In part it is a case of self-mastery. I am a world-citizen and have the personal freedom of the world. I have a right to ride third-class if I wish, and help all the others in that part of the ship to the same intelligence and freedom I have. Then will there finally be but one class? No; there will be several classes of accommodation that freemen may choose, but the scorn for the person who can not or will not spend so much for luxuries will be gone. Then more people will live within their means courageously and cheerfully. Then there will be less strife for wealth, because life's needs can be met for a reasonable sum of money and effort. I repeat here that equality in this world is neither possible nor desirable, but fairness and justice are both possible and practical. When there are more people with a world-vision, and more who are self-masters, the age of universal fairness will hasten its pace.

Here is one phase of world-vision. I do not use liquor, tobacco, tea, or coffee. You use all these in moderation, and you intend to keep on using them. Well, we can still find a common platform to stand on, and it is this: Call in the best scientific knowledge and the full contributions from the fields of business and religion, and then let us guide the education and training of the next generation by their best obtainable verdict and principles. That is fair; that is world-vision applied. You may say I have no right to interfere with your private habits. Perhaps not, if you lived on a planet alone; but if your private habits teach my boys to be slaves to vices, then it is different. The tax-payer has a right to a voice in the habits of others when those habits increase his taxes. All I ask now is a true verdict from all the sources of knowledge on any subject. Let prejudice and personal preference step aside and let the truth rule.

If I had one supreme wish regarding humanity, it would be that every child born into this world should be intelligent and capable, and then trained to be honest and made free in his own sphere. You say that is impossible? It is not too high as an aim, and I can labor as though I expected it to come, and thus live in such a world in my own mind. It is a world-principle to favor everything that makes men free and independent, and to oppose everything that puts one class in the power of another. Congo rum means bondage to the natives, and the man who will neither make rum for the Congo, nor ship it there, is a better neighbor than the one who will.

A NARROW VISION.

There are those who say it is not the world's affair how they live, if they have the money to pay for their luxuries. One question is, "How did they get so much money?" Waiving that question, remember this, my Master and yours had a right to all kinds of luxuries, but to win a world He gave up His rights and lived with the common people in their simple way. With Him it was an estimate of values. The conduct of Christ can be defended from the pure business standpoint of working for what was worth most in the long run. His was a world-vision, with all its requirements and privileges. His course was not a necessity, except that right means are always a necessity for reaching the best results. I have no right to spend on luxuries and personal indulgence more than the majority of those who prepare those luxuries can afford to spend, provided they live as sensibly as I do. This must include their parents also, for one generation starts its successor for well or ill, and every life must be measured by including its very foundation. The sins of the father may leave his child with an unfair chance, compared with the well-born.

Electricity is just the same to-day as it was five hundred years ago. The knowledge and use of electricity have greatly increased since then. Human nature and its needs are the same to-day as they were five hundred years ago, yet the possibility of supplying human needs has greatly multiplied. There are many in position to help apply these better methods for the benefit of the masses, but they will not, and yet they use all modern helps for their own self-gratification. There is need of a strong public sentiment to prod such persons into the traces and compel them to do their share of the work. Humanity can not exist in its present crowded state without a great deal of labor, study, and care. Unless disabled in some way, it would seem impossible to excuse any person from doing his part. He could not be excused by birth, for no person could claim greater privileges than the Son of God Himself, yet He said, "My Father worketh hitherto, and I work." Not all at the same task, but every creature at some task, is the rule of our being. The aristocrat, whose parents taught him that he was a grandee, and must not work, is being crowded to the wall, and the sooner the better. That has been a part of the bad teaching in Spain, and unfortunately Spain is not the only country where laziness has been called a virtue.

I was standing on the summit of a high hill south of Fiesole, greatly enjoying the extended view of the valley of the Arno, with the city of Florence and the mountains beyond. I thought, what wars and struggles this valley has witnessed in the attempt of one man or one set of men to rule others and become their masters! I stand and view this valley with greater dreams of world-conquest than Alexander ever had—he never conquered himself. Mine begins with myself, and then aims to teach the whole world the possibility and joy of self-conquest as the only sure road to world-conquest. Alexander gained his victories only with the aid of many others; I likewise gain by the help of others. I have seen more of the world than he, by far, and I have possessed its beauty and enjoyed its privileges. Thus the world is at my feet to do what I want done, provided I am first at my own feet and can do for myself what I ought to do. Christ did not refuse world-conquest; it was only the devil's way of accomplishing it that He rejected. He knew a far better way, and adopted it, and He urges men to follow His example. Strange and insane as it may seem, the leaders of the world, who might know better, have accepted the devil's offer and vainly tried to work his plan. If the devil ever laughs, he might be pardoned for laughing at the folly of many men called Great. It is too serious in its consequences for any mirth on the part of ourselves, who have so much at stake. My dream of world-conquest would bring every human being to sit at the feet of the Great Teacher and learn how He conquered Himself, and how He will yet conquer the whole world. He said to His followers, "I have called you friends." World-conquest by Jesus means that He is to have all the inhabitants of the world as His friends. If His friends, of course all will be friends of each other, and all will be your friends and mine. Is that prize not worth the cost that falls to your lot and mine to pay? The Redeemer thought it was, and He paid far more than is asked of any one of us to-day.

"FLORENCE, ITALY, April 30th, 5.30 A. M.

" 'We who are about to die salute you.' These were the words formerly spoken by strong, brave men in the Roman arena to proud, ignoble slaves perched on the seats above them. Slaves? Yes, to every vice known to the rich, pampered, degenerate aristocracy of pagan Rome. Dressed in sumptuous robes and rich adornment, they were so base at heart as to enjoy seeing those noble men from the mountains and plains butcher each other like demons. How is such degradation possible? Simply by training the young to low tastes and beastly amusements. A child easily learns to be kind or cruel. This can be seen in neighboring houses in the way different children treat their pet animals. How can the kings and generals of to-day be so ready to send men to kill each other in battle? They have been trained to do it, that is the explanation. The Roman arena now lies in ruins, a thing to interest the curious traveler, and its particular barbarities are no more. Its spirit, however, still survives in all too vigorous a form, not only in war, but also in business and society.

"There is a far better salutation to-day: 'We who are about to live a larger life salute you. We who have entered the arena for world-conquest salute you. To every son and daughter of earth who is young enough to grow, we call to you, "Come into the great arena and let us conquer the world, not for us alone, but for itself." ' This is the last great battlefield in the world's long history of war—the last, the greatest, and the most glorious. It is the greatest and the most glorious because every person is to be enlisted and every one is to become a world-conqueror. Nothing less than a world-vision will do for the leaders in this conquest. What is the aim to be reached? To train the childhood of the whole world into strong, intelligent, useful men and women—to give every child of the world a fair chance. Conquest? Yes, each to conquer his own world and become master of himself and his surroundings. The smallest and weakest may enter this arena; no exclusions because of size, sex, race, or lineage. Only one condition is required; each combatant must have life and purpose enough to desire to grow. When a province seeks independence from its sovereign country, it starts a revolution and seeks recognition from other independent powers. You need to do the same. The only powers you need consider are yourself and God. God's recognition was contained in the type of your creation, namely: His own image. God created you with possibilities of a self that can think and act and keep your own thoughts and purposes in spite of everything. By your creation He gave you recognition as a world-power and made you worthy to become a world-conqueror. It remains only for you to secure your own recognition of yourself as worthy to become an independent world-power. Step into the arena. We who are about to live as world-conquerors with a world-vision, salute you, and with you the coming generations.

"The first step toward victory is to prepare to serve yourself and others. You must put out of your own world what does not belong there. You must put into it what does belong there. God and any other helps to conquest belong there. No one is ever independent of his friends and helpers, any more than he is independent of his feet and hands. Do not make the blunder of thinking you can ever run away from God and your friends. A soldier who runs away from his friends has gone among his enemies, where none will help him. A conqueror must have help, and securing that help, securing an army, is the first act.

"What are the boundaries of this world you are to conquer? It has none unless you set them up. If you are God's child, you can roam over all your Father's premises. Your thought and your vision may mount to the highest point and travel to the remotest star, or they may descend and wallow in any filth near you. You can guard swine, feed with them, and be unworthy of their company, or you can guard swine and really live among the stars. I have seen a boy watching an open gate to keep the cattle from going through. With a book in his hands, he was living among the sages, learning of them, and acquiring a vision that had no bounds. His world-to-be had a center, and he was that center; its circumference was too far away to be measured. It is possible for every individual to become too great to think a mean thought or purposely do a mean act to himself or any other being. Would it not be a joy to live among such world-conquerors? Christ thought so and gave His life and service to win and make possible just such a future world as that. Just such a neighborhood as that I like to think, and then remember that that neighborhood has the same boundaries as God's universe. None need ever fear he will stumble against those boundaries. He may grow as large as he will, his vision reach infinity, and yet there is room, for God is still beyond, and He says, 'Come!' Is it not worth while?"

This was the vision that came to me almost word for word that early April morning in Florence. In sunny Italy one can find both stars and filth—I mean moral filth. There are those who, if they do not easily find filth ready-made, order some with their money. If one does that, his eagle has clipped his pinions and dropped into a dungeon, no longer a king, but a captive. In my travels in many lands I lived in the star-realm. I saw many traveling on a much lower plane, yet both were open to their choice. I wish I might close that lower passage and leave only the upper one open. You can do it for yourself if you will.

GREAT PRINCIPLES.

I seek in these world-studies to learn what are the great underlying principles and laws of growth and development which are of universal application. I seek those that defy monopoly and exclusiveness; I am sure God has made man for such universal freedom as this would mean. No person has any right to hold for his exclusive use, or for his family and followers, any general good or benefit which he will neither sell nor give to the world at large after a reasonable period of monopoly. Patents and copyrights are such, and are by law limited to a certain period of years. If there is anything in apostolic succession or any religious rite that is of any value, it is time these were freely offered to all denominations, to be used in their own way as they see fit. All this must be done without asking them to march in the

217

procession of any earthly leader, wear his colors, or admit his superiority. For him to longer refuse the free gift of these so-called privileges is to convict him either of extreme selfishness and greed for power or of being false in claiming virtue in what is only a fraud. If he is honest and is bound by tradition, it is time such chains were broken. The Christian world does an act of kindness to break that chain and arouse such an ecclesiastical Rip Van Winkle from his bondage of sleep.

I speak no word against the Catholic Church. That little group of old men at Rome, called the Vatican, is a thing entirely outside of the church. It is radically wrong in principle, as it is a power that seeks to master the world by ruling others, whereas Christ came to equip each person to rule himself.

The world will be obliged to repudiate all interference from Rome, both in governmental and religious affairs. The people and the local clergy of any country constitute the church in that country, and are intelligent enough to manage all their affairs without foreign interference. The church is wise to consider advice and suggestions from all sources, but all despotic rule, such as the Vatican attempts, must be rejected.

FAITH AND BELIEF IN WORLD-VISION.

It is very important to the seeker after a world-vision to have a large faith in God and humanity. He must believe in the general integrity of history and of men. He must be a believer rather than a doubter; better believe too much than too little. The world has slight use for a set of men whose first aim is to hunt for fraud and become professional critics. All students who seek for the truth have an eye open for error. They do not eat nuts, shells and all; they discriminate. Their aim, however, is to search for truth, and their attitude is that of believers. They say all is good until proved bad, whereas the habitual critic says all is bad until proved good. The seeker for truth makes a better traveling companion than the seeker for error; the believer is better than the doubter. I should like to live in a world of believers; a world of doubters would be a dreary place. One of the charms of children is their spirit of belief. A skeptical child, who doubts you and what you say, is not attractive; we want a child to be hopeful, large-hearted, optimistic, seeing our best side first. It is a part of world-vision not only to see far, but to trust far and believe far. The more I travel and the more I come in close touch with the busy people of different countries, the greater is my faith in humanity; I get a broader vision and a broader faith. It is impossible to see how people who do not believe much in God or men can call themselves liberal. They are narrow and ungenerous. They would narrow down my world so much that I could not live in it. Give me the true breadth and liberality of a large belief.

OUR DEBT TO OTHERS.

We people in America have had room to develop and grow. New fields, free institutions, and general education have greatly favored us. Southern Europe is the reverse of this. The tyranny of the past: cramped quarters, low wages, little public education, and most of the favors kept by the few in power of Church and State—have made a poor soil for growth. While we enjoy their art, music, and historic landmarks, we owe them more than the mere payment of hotel and railway bills, and the purchase of some art works; we owe them an example of our best Christian, American manhood and womanhood. Their wine and low amusements are the curse of the country, and our example should teach them this fact.

Every one who has either knowledge or property owes something to future generations. It is a part of world-vision to care whether the children of remote peoples are fairly treated or not. Inasmuch as the civilized part of the world profits greatly by the cheap labor of the more primitive people in the tropics and distant regions, we are, by the demands of honesty and justice, under obligation to give them the benefit of our better knowledge and civilization. We owe it to ourselves, as at present our sons who go among them are too often corrupted by the easy access to vice. With the present rapid intercourse of commerce and travel we shall either lift them up, or they will drag us down. Barbarians have conquered nations more civilized than themselves in the past, and it might be repeated. This world is like a human body: one part can not rob another without ultimate harm to itself. The child-races of the world must be given a fair chance.

Some line of helpfulness to the future is a most fruitful field for the independent worker who prefers to direct his own movements and pay his own bills. I hope many persons with some leisure time and some spare means may look for places of investment in this field.

CHAPTER XVII

SELF-MASTERY JOURNEYS

The Great Teacher says: "I am among you as he that serveth."
Therefore we believe: It is more honorable to sweep a floor than
it is to get it dirty. There are some well-dressed people whose laziness and false pride cause them to make unnecessary dirt for others to
clean up.

My first journey for special world-study began from my
old home, Baraboo, Wisconsin, in September, 1905. There
my wife and I parted: she to go to Duluth, to make a home
for our boy, and I to follow the sun on his westward way.
I had already studied three years in the universities of
Europe, and possessed a fair knowledge of German and
French; so with three languages and some experience in
travel in other lands, I felt well able to find my way.

After a brief stay in Madison, and another in Chicago,
I found myself hurrying on to Denver. What was of most
interest to me in that region was Judge Lindsay and his
work for the boys. I called on him and explained my er-
rand. He was very courteous, gave me much information,
and invited me to visit the juvenile court. The court-room,
with Judge Lindsay in the center, a group of boys who had
in some way come in touch with the court, and the probation
officers and several teachers from the school all gathered
around him, made a picture I shall not soon forget. What
were the judge and his co-workers doing? They were helping those boys to become men. I have been in various court-
rooms where trials were going on, and I have been in many
prisons in different parts of the world. One must at times
feel that there is a degree of hardness in the manner of

the officials. I have never been a prison official, and hence do not claim to know just what manner is best; but in Judge Lindsay's court there was an air of kindliness that helped me to believe more in humanity. Among the boys was one of eight or ten years, to whom the judge talked a little while, and then passed him on. The boy waited near by and began to cry, wiping his eyes with his hands. Before long all the cases had been disposed of, and the judge turned to this boy and said: "Come here, boy. What are you crying for? Is it because you did wrong, or is it because you were found out?" The boy replied, "It is because I did wrong." And from his manner I could not doubt his word. The judge had touched the real boy, and there was something to build on. Many a father could well take pattern of Judge Lindsay in the manner of meeting his own boys and of holding their confidence. I have visited juvenile courts in other cities, and am glad to say that the spirit of brotherly kindness is coming in. A fair and honest spirit is greatly needed in all criminal and other courts.

Salt Lake City was my next stopping-place. I wished to see and learn what I could of Mormonism. I spent an evening with one of the Twelve Apostles. He was very affable and seemed glad of the chance to vindicate his position of having two wives and being one of the leaders of Mormonism. This man, like many others, is really two persons: the man, and the Mormon. I found the man that evening; he was friendly and courteous. The Mormon— well, he was a Mormon; that describes him, and it seems the Mormon usually rules. I have varied experiences in seeking information of all sorts of persons. Sometimes I find the man, and sometimes I do not—only the official is visible; the man is so small that he can be completely hidden behind the mere name of an office; it matters little what the office may be. Fortunately, however, there are many instances in which I find the man.

The Mormon commercial building had a symbolic representation of the two noted places of the hereafter. "Holiness to the Lord" is cut in a tablet in the front of the upper story, while beneath, in the large show-window, were a lot of bottles of whisky arranged in artistic order. It was a very good symbol of heaven and hell, and judging from the number of saloons in Salt Lake City, one must conclude that the latter place was getting about all the traffic.

Next I moved on to San Francisco, to repeat the same methods of study. Salt Lake City and San Francisco, at that time, illustrated the extremes of high and low license, as the former was $100 per month and the latter $7. There seemed to be an unreasonable amount of drinking in both places. From San Francisco I sailed on the *Manchuria* for Yokohama *via* Honolulu. Mr. W. J. Bryan was on the same ship, and it was my privilege to make his acquaintance. I met him several times afterward, as we both took the same general course. It is easy to find the man in Mr. Bryan: he is larger than the politician and the orator, though these are by no means small.

At Honolulu I first visited the postoffice, then the schools; I wanted to see the children. In the public kindergarten there were five nationalities side by side: American, Hawaiian, Chinese, Japanese, and Portuguese. They sang a little song, in which the word "good-bye" in each of these languages was the leading idea in one of the five verses. Thus they all sang good-bye to the Americans, and to each of the others in turn. The whole world needs just such a lesson as that. Let all the children sing "good-bye" or "good morning" to the rest of the world for a few years, with the thought, "we wish you well," and strife and war will cease.

On the ship there were about fifty missionary people of various countries, denominations, and kinds of work. Conferences were held every day after leaving Honolulu, and here I learned a great deal about the people of the Orient, and especially the excellent spirit of those who go to carry the light of the gospel and civilization to the less favored parts of the earth.

I spent forty-five days in Japan and traveled fifteen hundred miles by rail, touching the chief cities, and made a trip into the interior, visiting temples, missions, schools, and prisons. I procured a little book with English and Japanese words and phrases, with the Japanese so well spelled out in English that I could usually read the word or sentence so as to be understood. Years of language-study give one facility in catching the sound of a foreign word. I talked by signs a good deal, and found the Orientals rather quick to understand that language. The institutions visited in Japan included the missions of a number of different denominations, a theological school of the Buddhists, where their priests are trained, and a number of high-schools, where I gave addresses. I visited the lower grades also, and often watched the children as they passed out or into the school-grounds. They were never rude to me, and never tried to be smart, as I fear some American boys would have done to a Japanese.

I found Korea a very interesting country. The dignified men with their long, white garments and odd hats, traveling in single file along the country-paths, looked at a distance like a cemetery with marble statues. Their cemeteries are usually rounded mounds of earth on the hillside, in a spot chosen by the soothsayers. I rode fourteen hours in a third-class car, and found the accommodations comfortable, and felt myself quite at home among the people. I went as far north as Seoul, and then returned on Thanksgiving Day to the southern port. I enjoyed my simple dinner on the train, observing the Korean people and landscape as a sort of dressing. Some Korean dates, strung on a stick and dried, furnished an agreeable dessert.

I took my last look at Japan from the steamer-deck in the harbor of that beautiful bay at Nagasaki. I carried with me a store of pleasant memories of Japan and her people as the steamer plowed the waters on her way to China. Shanghai has two cities side by side. The old, within the walls, is dingy and dirty, crowded and curious. The new city is foreign in appearance and is built of substantial brick. Here the Orient and the Occident meet, and I am sorry some of our Western people do not set a better example of moral and Christian conduct before the people in whose midst they go for trade or travel.

Foo Chow—one part new, where the foreigner lives, on the hills; and the other part old, where China can be seen and felt on streets only wide enough for eight or ten men to walk abreast—has impressed many pictures on my mind. A great variety of articles are made in little shops on both sides of the street. I bought some needles from a man who made them by hand; they are rude, but they will sew. I called at Amoy and Swatow, and then on I went to Hong Kong, the only Westerner on the ship. The latter city, seen from its spacious harbor, is grand by night or by day. A man with his wife and daughter rowed me far out to the ship in their sampan house-boat. These people live in their boats, and some of them keep a pig in a crate across the back end of the boat. I leaned over the side of the ship to see them eat their simple meal, but the woman looked up at me in a reproving way, as though it annoyed her to have me looking on, so I moved farther away. These people were plain and primitive, but they impressed me as doing the best they could under the dead weight of old tradition and the ruling classes, who do nothing for them.

The mosquitoes and the sun both gave me a warm welcome to the Philippines. A mosquito-net canopy and one sheet was all I required as a night-covering in that sunny land, even in January. The Americans whom I met were very friendly, and I found the schools full of interesting children, all studying our text-books in the English language. My way led me back to Hong Kong in order to get a ship for Singapore. If you wish to get warm, go to Singapore. You will be about one degree from the equator, and the sun is cordial in its greeting. I had a delightful ride on the electric tram that runs out into the country. It was then almost a jungle, but man drives back the jungle. My next stop was at Penang. In these waters the men and boys seem as much at home as porpoises, and dive after coins for the amusement of travelers. Boat-loads of beautiful shells and corals were offered for sale. I took some delightful rides, with a young American of the mission, in a double jinrikisha drawn by an enterprising Chinaman. The cocoanut and other forests of that region are grand, and the vegetation is luxuriant.

Then we turned northward, and the cool breeze we met as we neared Calcutta was very welcome. India is rich in interest; it is not easy to pass so lightly over it all. It was new to me to see six men carrying a piano on their heads, and to see men wade out into a pond and wash and drink in the same water. They stand there and wash clothes on a granite slab, and throw them to a sheet on the bank. I went on northward and stopped at Pacur, Benares, and Allahabad. At Philibhit I met an old schoolmate, and here I had a ride on an elephant, and also on a camel. I had a most magnificent view of the great Himalaya snowy range; a very rare sight, as the air is usually hazy. I stopped at Bareilly and at Agra, where I saw that most marvelous building of the world, the Taj Mahal, both by day and by moonlight. At Muttra the fire-worshipers were a fascinating study. At evening they place candles on little boards and set them afloat on the river. On the stone steps that led to the river, a fat, sacred cow was standing, and a sacred monkey was climbing over her back and swinging from her tail. In many cases it is better to be a monkey in India than a woman. Delhi, with its ruins of Mohammedan misrule, is well worth a visit. Now I find myself hurrying on towards Bombay. The English railway officials are very accommodating. England is doing very much for the people of this land. The nabobs of India, who used to live in barbaric splendor at the expense of the common people, would like to have the country to themselves again. So would the same class of politicians in the Philippines like to rule that country. It would be too much of a game of fox-and-geese; in either case there would be a few fat foxes and a lot of lean geese. The people of neither of these countries are yet able to protect themselves against bad rulers. We remember that even in Western lands the people have a struggle to hold their own against corrupt rule. The missionaries of the various denominations are doing a great work for India, and Christian education makes excellent men and women of the people there.

I was in the company of several missionaries on the ship that carried us from Bombay through the Red Sea to Port Said. The Suez Canal allows one to see something of the desert by water. A wonderful mirage lingered for quite a time in view, and was very real in its resemblance to a bay with projecting land.

At Cairo I first saw the Nile. On the bridge I met camels bearing new-mown clover, and it almost made me homesick. I never ate strawberries that tasted so delicious as some wild ones the boys were selling in little leaf-baskets. I was thirsty, and bought them; and there, in sight of the Pyramids, I ate wild strawberries and thought of my boyhood. The next day I went out to the Pyramids and climbed to the summit of the great Gizeh.

It was Easter-time, and many pilgrims were on their way to Jerusalem, but I had to be content with a short stay in Palestine. I had planned to see the northern part and Damascus, but the rough sea would not let the small boats go out to the ships; so after waiting several days at Jaffa, I went back to Cairo, and from there by rail to Alexandria. Our ship had a good many people bound for Athens, to attend the Grecian games. I reached Constantinople on Easter Sunday. There is much to say of the people in that city, their shops, bazaars, and mosques; of the latter, St. Sophia being the most important. To describe my trip up the Bosphorus and do it justice would be a difficult task. It is grand, romantic, and varied. Robert College, in a picturesque situation, is one of the valuable friends of better things in Turkey. It is a great window through which Christian light is entering that dark land of the False Prophet.

My next move was northward. There was a good deal of formality in getting permission to leave Turkey. The police examined my passport a number of times and at various points. I stopped at Philippopolis, Belgrade, and Buda Pest on my way to Vienna. Then continuing, I visited Prague and Dresden, and remained a longer time at Leipzig, where I had been a student in the university some years before. Erelong I was again in Berlin. Germany has grown rich and showy. The former simplicity of clothing has given way to more expensive attire. I think Germany has lost something valuable in this regard.

I was delighted with a trip through Denmark, Sweden, and Norway, reaching as far north as Christiania. Some parts of Sweden reminded me very much of Wisconsin. These home-like pictures greet me with a peculiar charm as they flash upon me unawares. I was surprised with such a picture in the Philippines, where the fields, flowers, and weeds of January so much resemble early September in Wisconsin.

I next took my way across North Germany, into Holland and Belgium, and then to Paris, where I was somewhat at home because of having been a student there. I do not travel nights: one sees nothing at that time. I plan to reach some convenient place before night, and rest for the next day. I go out on the streets in the evening and study the people, and see how they spend their leisure time—this is important. I chat a few minutes with the policeman, the cabman, the shop-keeper, the lounger on the corner, or any one I meet. I ask the way to some point, drop into a church, step into a café or restaurant, and glance around as though looking for some one, as indeed I am: I am looking for everybody and at everything. I never step into a dive; I do not care to see humanity at its worst: I see enough as I travel along the decent paths of traffic. Above all, I do not want to see woman at her worst. The selfishness of the men is to blame for her degradation. We men can change all this if we have a mind to. The women will do their part and lend a little extra help to us as soon as we are willing to start house-cleaning.

I spent a longer time in England, as there is much to learn from these our relatives by blood and language. From Liverpool I sailed to New York. After stopping there a few days, I made a brief visit at Washington, from which city I went directly to Chicago, and then to Baraboo.

The time consumed in this trip was one year. The distance traveled was thirty thousand miles. The cost in money was, on the average, within $70 per month, or a little over $800 for the whole trip.

Let me now give several other tests of the possibility of being comfortable while seeing much of the world at moderate cost. In September, 1910, my wife and I started from our home in Wisconsin on a long journey to study humanity. On this trip, also, we did not travel nights, except on the water; there we drew the line and stayed by the ship day and night. We stopped at Louisville, Ky., and at Nashville, Tenn., and from there we went to Talladega, Ala., where our son was superintendent of a college-farm for colored students. My wife remained in his home while I took a tour through Alabama and Georgia, studying schools and prisons, and also the color problem. I talked with prison and government officials, with editors, professional and business men, and any one I could find who knew that country. I gave addresses in churches and schools wherever an opportunity offered, but avoided giving any advice on the color problem; in this I was a student, not a teacher.

We visited Mobile, and then went our way through the pines and moss-covered forests to New Orleans. We were especially interested in the French quarter, where we wandered about with the feeling that we were in France again, where we had been together years before. It seems strange that this section has kept its French character so long in an American city. It shows that people can follow different customs from their neighbors if they wish to. Humanity is not compelled to follow either a wise or an unwise course; a community can be a desert in the midst of an oasis or an oasis in the midst of a desert, the world affords examples of both.

Havana contains many things that are new and strange. The Cubans have a future, and I believe they will redeem themselves when certain changes take place in the way of better opportunities. From Havana we sailed to Vera Cruz, the port I so well remembered from my geography days.

Our next call was at Orizaba, where, because of the temporary absence of a teacher in the Methodist mission-school, we were privileged to keep house in rooms in the mission building. All the other occupants of the building were Mexicans, and they were good neighbors. We spoke enough Spanish to get along with the people and to do all our marketing. We bought bread, meat, fruit, vegetables, and everything we used, just as others did, in the public markets. I have done this everywhere in my extensive travels, and there is no way to make the acquaintance with the people of any country like buying in their markets in small quantities, as they do, and using their own language. I did not often pay more than the people did, for I took pains to learn the prices by asking at several places. I believe in all my travels in foreign countries, now covering nearly six years, and almost the whole time buying my food directly in the shops and markets, I have very rarely paid more than the usual price paid by the people themselves.

We made a somewhat longer stay in Puebla and Mexico City, which included a delightful sojourn in Cuernavaca. Returning to Puebla, my wife secured board in the Methodist mission-school, where she remained two months, and then sailed for New York.

February 22, 1911, I started southward from Puebla. It was a journey full of interest, which I should like to describe in detail if space permitted. As my object is to give the results of my studies of humanity and the lessons learned from many lands, I shall follow only the outlines of the voyage.

Tropical forests and scenery have a wonderful charm for me. The jungle is a marvel of growth; the vines reach out vigorously and twine over the trees, while the curious flowers, the magnificent palms, and a thousand pictures greet the traveler in passing through the hills and forests.

I sailed from Salina Cruz, the southern port of Mexico, to Acajutla, the port of San Salvador. Here, at the capital of that little republic, I was fortunate in striking the time of the inauguration of the new president, when a gala day brought many people in from the country and from other towns. I was informed, on good authority, that a number of the leaders of the defeated party were entertained in the prison for a few days at this time, "to insure domestic tranquillity and secure the blessings of liberty to the people." Preventive is sometimes better than cure in the body politic, as well as in other bodies.

From Acajutla I took a ship of the Pacific Mail bound for Panama. This ship called at all the principal ports, bringing flour and manufactured articles, and carrying away coffee and other tropical products. I thus had a good opportunity to see and learn much of the people. Sixteen days in the Canal Zone afforded me a very fair idea of the general situation and the problems to be solved. No one can study that canal with an open mind without feeling a deep respect and reverence for God and the humanity He has created. It proved to me that if man can do so much for the material progress, he can do as much for the moral, the physical, and the spiritual welfare of the whole race of mankind; nothing less than this will suffice. The authorities do not allow yellow fever to get a foothold on the zone. The authorities the world over can banish moral diseases and make a canal zone of the whole earth, so soon as they make that an aim, as is now done in reference to the fever at the Panama Canal. It struck me as a marvelous thing that science could stamp out yellow fever and make sanitary conditions there so good. I call it the greatest case of divine healing I have ever known. It was divine healing because it was all done by the use of the intelligence, the materials, and the appliances that Divinity has placed within man's reach. Divine healing must be permanent, and in the power of those concerned, that they may guard against future danger. The engineering project of cutting a path for the ships through a mountain, of tearing down the everlasting hills, and carrying them away to build an enormous dam and such gigantic locks, touched the very depths of my nature. As I looked upon it all I was stirred with the deepest emotion, and the words of the psalmist came to my mind:

"When I consider Thy heavens, the work of Thy fingers,
The moon and the stars, which Thou hast ordained;
What is man, that Thou art mindful of him?
And the son of man, that Thou visitest him?
For Thou hast made him but little lower than the angels,
And crownest him with glory and honor.
Thou madest him to have dominion over the works of Thy hands;
Thou hast put all things under his feet:
All sheep and oxen, yea, and the beasts of the field;
The fowl of the air, and the fish of the sea,
Whatsoever passeth through the paths of the seas."

I took a deck passage from Colon to Kingston, Jamaica, and rode among the people of the West Indies, who are helping to build the canal. I thought if I could ride through the canal they built, I could ride with them on the same deck. Most of them were colored, but there were also other races represented. There was but little profanity or rudeness of any kind; they were courteous to each other and to me. They sang hymns, but did not engage in gambling. The latter is far too common on ship-board, from the first cabin downwards. I spent some time on the Island of Jamaica, and then sailed to Santiago, Cuba. I traveled westward, stopping at Christo, Bayamo, Camaguay, and Matanzas, thus getting a very good idea of this beautiful island of palms. At Havana I took the steamer for Florida, and thence went northward to Washington, to rejoin my wife. I traveled by short stages, stopping to make further acquaintance with the people and conditions in the Atlantic States.

This journey from Puebla, México, south to the Isthmus, and north through the West Indies to Washington, covered a distance, including sidetrips, of five thousand miles. It occupied three months' time, and cost $180, or $60 per month. I was entirely comfortable all the way, and I believe I got more information and more satisfaction out of the trip than the average traveler who pays far more for his privileges.

The next instance of economic traveling included two persons. On July 7, 1911, my wife and I started from Beach Haven, N. J., where we had spent a few pleasant weeks with friends, to make a European trip. We sailed from New York on the Anchor Line for Londonderry, Ireland. I wanted to get better acquainted with the Irish people, and there were many of them all around us on the ship. We sat among them, ate with them, talked with them, like one big family on that ocean voyage. We spent six weeks in Ireland; two weeks in Londonderry and its environs; one in Belfast; one in Dublin, and two weeks in Cork. We had rooms with private families all the way, spending only one night at a hotel. This is our rule everywhere, for in this way we get better acquainted with the people, and it is far less expensive.

From Cork we sailed to Fishguard, Wales, and thence to Cardiff. We wished to learn something of the mines and the mining region. Now when the coal warms me, or generates the steam that drives the engine of ship or railway on which I ride so comfortably, I think of the men who go far down into the dingy mines to get that coal for me. Would that the careless, well-fed, and well-groomed world might take more time to think of those who make their luxuries possible! I talked with some of the men whose faces were as black as the coal with its dust; they were just like other men. I stood and watched the crowds going into the mines and those coming out; they were just like other men and boys, and I felt a kindly sympathy for them all. What did arouse my wrath against the brewers were the enormous vans with their monster loads of beer sent to catch the money of these men as they come out from the mines. I saw a lot of broken windows from a late strike. One cause of that strike was that the men did not have money enough for their needs. One reason for lack of money was that they had spent it for drink, and the brewers were teaching them to drink more, and telling them it was necessary for their strength.

From Cardiff, we next stopped at Plymouth, and visited the place from which the *Mayflower* sailed to New England. From England we sailed to capture Brittany, landing at Brest. The old and the new brush against each other on the streets of this curious city, when the quaint, full peasant costumes meet the skirts so narrow that the wearers could step only ten or twelve inches. We stopped at Quimper, and saw the fine old cathedral, and at Nantes, where we visited the churches of note, and the castle in which was signed the famous Edict of Nantes. La Rochelle was the last stronghold of the Huguenots. Its fine sea beach and the beautiful park adjoining make it a favorite resort in the summer. We spent a longer time at Bordeaux, and made several trips into the country to visit the vineyards for which that region is noted. This was the fourth time my feet had trodden French territory. That France can be what she is after losing so many of her best citizens in her past history, convinces me of the vigor and force of her people.

From Bayonne we crossed the border and were at last on Spanish soil. San Sebastian is a favorite summer resort of the royal family of Spain, and is surely a charming place, with fine views of sea and land. Hotels are not found near the railway stations in Spain; in fact, in some cities, they are far away. It was our custom for my wife to remain at the station while I went to find a private room. Thus I had no baggage with me, and was free to go on if the first place did not suit. My experience is that one can usually find what he wants if he knows where to look for it. In these searches for rooms I learned to know the people, and I was also practicing the language.

At Burgos we found a wonderful old cathedral and curious streets and scenes. In the evening crowds of people thronged the broad arcade extending around a square in the center of the city. They were strolling, chatting vigorously, and looking at each other; the men admiring the women and the women admiring the men. Men and women do not mingle as freely in Spanish countries as with us, so they do a good deal of looking when occasion offers. That seemed to be the principal aim at the services in the churches on Easter Sunday in Santiago, Cuba. In one fine church I saw just one old man among the men giving close attention to his prayer-book, the rest were looking at the women.

Valladolid was our next place of sojourn. This city has many historical associations, and the square is still shown where heretics used to be burned. The fine old churches are not well attended now. An interesting ride of 155 miles took us to the capital through a region whose soil is not very fertile. Large groves of pine trees trimmed with thick, bushy tops were passed—turpentine is a product of these pines. We found the people friendly with each other and also with us. They seemed to get acquainted very easily and to find fluent topics of conversation. They carried lunches with them, as we did, and they offered food and wine to each other. We declined the wine with all the Spanish politeness at our command, but the foreigner is at a disadvantage because of the numerous complimentary words and phrases that are hard to manage. Zigzagging back and forth, I traveled 1,400 miles in Spain on third class cars and had no occasion to find any fault with the treatment I received from the people. The common people of this country have never had a fair chance—public schools and general opportunities of improvement have been lacking.

Madrid is building rapidly, but rooms are small and crowded, and rent is high. They say old buildings are torn down faster than new ones are put up. There are few if any small houses such as are so common in Ireland and England. We always see the noted art galleries and museums in the different cities we visit, and of course those of Madrid are very fine. We also saw the king and queen as they drove out of the palace. Those in position to know speak well of them; they say the king works faithfully for his country, and seems to be gaining the confidence of his subjects, while the priests are surely losing their hold upon the people.

Granada and the Alhambra are two words that have a charm in their sound because of the wonderful writings of Washington Irving. The tram carries one through a magnificent forest to the top of the hill near the castle. This forest covers a number of acres, showing what Spain might have had in timber had her rulers in Church and State given more care to tree-culture and less time to exterminating the Moors and stamping out heresy by means of the Inquisition. We spent two months at Seville, and occupied a private room where the tower of the cathedral swept its shadow across our southern window every day. This tower, called the Giralda, is a relic of Moorish times, and from its lofty summit one has a wide view over the plains. Most of the streets of Seville are very narrow; two donkeys loaded with panniers of bread can not pass at all points. New streets are now being cut through, and many houses fall before this modernizing process. The quaint features are giving way for newer ideas in all the cities I have visited.

Mrs. Smith remained at Seville while I took a journey into Portugal. These two countries have much in common, but I could not help noticing the absence of priests and nuns. The priests are very numerous in Spain, and easily recognized by their long, black gowns. In Portugal the republic has forbidden them to wear these gowns on the street, and now they can not be distinguished from other people. In Lisbon I had the privilege of addressing a large and attentive audience at the Y. M. C. A. rooms, the very able general secretary being my interpreter. The door is open for the gospel in Portugal, and the large attendance at the several services I visited shows good results for the mission work done there. Spain and Portugal must have more schools and the Bible to bring them up to a higher degree of advancement.

Gibraltar is a great fortress, especially interesting to us, as England and Spain were once rivals and about equal in power, while England now holds the key to the Mediterranean on the most strategic spot of the Spanish peninsula.

While I had seen something of Mohammedanism in the Orient and in Turkey, I wanted to become better acquainted with its workings, and also to study a French colony. We therefore sailed for Algiers, where we found a delightful winter climate. The Cross and the Crescent here meet, and the French Government undertakes to side with neither and to keep friends with both. I believe the way to test Islamism is to judge it by its treatment of women. The Mohammedan buys and sells his wives, shuts them up in a den or palace, whichever he may happen to have, and then by calling it his religion defends his conduct before the world. It is the disgrace of civilization that the mantle of religion has been allowed to cover so much human wrong and sin for centuries. Men commit the darkest crimes under that pretense, and then say it is their religion and it must not be interfered with. When one condemns their crimes, they are ready to "fight for their religion," as they choose to call it. If the world has anything more unjust, deceitful, and vile under the pretense of divine sanction, yet having a certain degree of culture, than Mohammedanism, it would be interesting to know what it is. The leaders of this false religion know better, and the civilized world should tell them so. Through the kindness of some missionaries, who are doing an excellent work among the women and girls, my wife had an opportunity to see something of the sad home life of Moslem women. It is too bad that France is teaching the Moslem to cultivate and drink wine, and thus robbing him of one of his few virtues. At the harbor of Algiers there are literally acres of ground covered with immense casks of wine, which is grown on rich soil that should be producing something better than strong drink. I must say this for the Arabs of Algiers, they make a good, honest loaf of bread which they dare sell by weight. It is not puffed up with wind to make it look large, as is too often the case here in America. The Arab has good material in him, his religion makes him bad; teach him the religion of Christ and he will become a good citizen.

After a pleasant stay of six weeks in Algiers, and a trip into the Kabyle Mountains, we sailed for Naples. We were right among the Italians and the Greeks who were returning from the Americas, where they had gone to work and earn money for their families. I talked with many of them, and all were very civil to me. What these people need is a fair chance to be educated and refined, and they will become good citizens. We owe something to the men who build our canals and railroads. We have left them too much to the saloonkeeper and to the low-grade politician.

After seeing Naples and its environs, including Vesuvius and Pompeii, we went on to Rome for Easter, then to Florence, Bologna, and Venice. I had been in Italy before, but my wife had not; and we moved on leisurely, as our time was entirely our own. From Venice we went northward to Trent, where we visited the church in which the famous Council of Trent was held. Leaving Italy, we passed through the romantic Tyrol to Innsbruck, and later to Munich. We had both been in Germany before, and felt quite at home with the people and the language.

By the time we reached Munich, I had traveled 9,500 miles and my wife 8,670 miles, in ten and one-half months. We had seen many of the principal cities and sights, and much of the people and their customs and modes of life. We had been entirely comfortable, and felt that our aim in travel had been more than met. All this was done by two persons at a total cost of $500. It was a further triumph of certain principles we had started out to test and prove. My next trip was into Russia. As Mrs. Smith did not care to take this long journey, she boarded for a time with the German Methodist Deaconesses while I was gone. The principal points I touched were Vienna, Warsaw, Vilna, and St. Petersburg. I rode third class, and found it very comfortable. The roadbed and the track are good, and the service also. The cars are plain, the seats are without cushions and wide enough to make a very good bed at night. It is the best accommodation for cheap railway travel I have seen in any part of the world; India comes next to it in my judgment. It would be an excellent plan to have plain cars for a cheaper price in America. We Americans who have more sense than dollars use third class cars in other countries; why should we not do the same in our own? Those in position to know the facts say they like the Russian people, but the government is oppressive and unfair to them. I fully concur in this verdict. Tradition in Church and State retards the progress of this vast country.

From St. Petersburg I went back to Vilna, then to Edyt-kuhnen, *en route* for Koenigsburg. Edytkuhnen is a little town on the border of Germany and Russia, and I wanted to observe the people on the border line of two such nations. I strolled out to the boundary, spoke with the guard, and stood on the line with both feet, then with one foot on either side. I had amused myself thus on the boundary between Germany and Austria. I thought how easy it would be for one of several persons in authority to set these neighbors on opposite sides of this artificial boundary to robbing and killing each other, and for what trivial reasons!

I felt much freer on German soil, I knew the language and required no pass; I paid nearly twice as much for some articles of food, however. From Koenigsburg I bought my ticket to Posen in order to see more of the Polish people. Poland has an interesting history and the world can profit by studying its details.

Berlin is a great and magnificent city. Like all the rest of Germany, it has changed very much since the time of my student days there. The people are forgetting their former simplicity of life. Once the students dressed very plainly, not so now; but the same is true of my own alma mater.

One month's time from the day I left Munich, I was walking along Schiller Street at nine o'clock at night look-ing for the house where my wife was living, or, in other words, I was looking for my home. In our travels we al-ways carried our home with us, for the material part of a home for two may be easily provided in most parts of the world if one knows how. The vital part is the harmonious spirits of one man and one woman, each bent on doing his part and demanding no more than his share. This is easy if the two know how, and have a mind to follow their knowledge. I would like to help all my young friends to the capacity and the power so needful in this field.

Now, what is the lesson from my Russian trip? Well, I beat myself this time; 2,900 miles, one month's time, traveling in entire comfort and getting a great deal out of my journey, and it cost me only $50. It is simple enough when one knows how and is master of himself.

Russia does this for her people that is truly commendable; she makes it possible for them to travel plainly at a very reasonable rate. Speed the day when America does the same! The public must not demand such luxurious cars, such rapid trains—dangerous to men and hard on the track—nor claim such exorbitant damages for accidents that can not be avoided nor foreseen. When both passengers and employees co-operate in protecting railway property, and in avoiding needless expense and waste, a long step will have been taken toward cheaper rates. This is one of the present economic problems.

The seventh of July, 1912, closed one year of travel for us. It is of interest to note the opportunities enjoyed and the expense incurred. I had traveled 12,425 miles, and my wife 8,670 miles. The cost of all this was $586. We call it $50 per month, which is within the facts.

From Munich we moved on to Wurtsburg, next to Frankfort-on-the-Main, and then to Cologne, as usual traveling by easy stages to see the country and the people.

Our ride down the Rhine, between the vine-covered hills, capped here and there with castles or romantic ruins, was delightful. Years before I had taken this trip as a student of language, now I was repeating it as a student of men.

We took the railway from Cologne to Arnhem, Holland, and afterwards spent a few days at The Hague and

Rotterdam. Then we went to Brussels, where we greatly enjoyed rambling among the historic buildings and museums. *Via* Ostend to London brought us once more on Britain's soil. It is easy to find good private rooms in British territory, and I feel very much at home there.

After spending some weeks in London, we sailed on the White Star Line from Southampton, touching at Cherbourg and Queenstown. We landed at New York and then took the steamer for Boston through the sound. Some things peculiar to that city were of especial interest to me. There is an Italian quarter where one fresh from Italy might easily think himself in the land of Garibaldi. We spent ten days in Boston, then pursued our journey *via* Montreal and Toronto to Chicago, and my old home in Wisconsin.

This last test of traveling cheaply and comfortably covered fourteen months' time; 19,000 miles of travel for myself and 15,400 for my wife, and cost us $800. For convenience we call it $60 per month, which is more than we used for all purposes.

The special things in view in my travels were schools, missions, religions and prisons. My aim was to study the institutions and customs that are helpful and also the causes and agencies that are harmful to humanity. To illustrate, here are people who are prosperous and good citizens. What has made them so, what is the lesson they have to teach the world? Again, here are people who are ignorant and wretched. Why are they so, and who is to blame? Are such conditions necessary, and can they not be shown a better way? I went to the prisons, saw the inmates, studied their faces and the expressions they carried, and then inquired what brought those men to that place. I asked how many convictions for this crime and for that, and why did these people commit those crimes. One does not learn everything, but he who travels far and wide with his mind open will learn a great deal about human nature—both its wrongs and its remedies.

CHAPTER XVIII

PERSONAL SKETCH

PREPARATION FOR THIS WORK.

THIS brief biography will contain only what can reasonably be demanded as the conditions under which every child should be brought into the world and trained for usefulness. The idea is not that every child should be thought of as a traveler, or a student of language, or any of my specialties, but that each should be trained into intelligent self-mastery, thrift, and honesty, and then let his own judgment and circumstances decide in what particular way he will employ his time and talent.

I was born with good health on a farm in Wisconsin, and in a Christian home. Farther back than I can remember, I was taught to obey my parents, wait on myself, and to work and help others. My earliest recollection is that these were natural things, and must be done as a matter of course. I well remember my mother saying to me, "Wait on yourself, and your friends will think the more of you." Wait on yourself was in the air of our home. I have many times been sorry for persons who have been taught laziness and dependence from infancy—a very good training for ciphers and anarchists. Instead of being taught to spend every cent for some trifle, I was taught to save my pennies for some good purpose. I never had a lot of money, and I can not remember any distinct fact before the occasion which brought me my first dollar. The carpenter had accidentally rolled a heavy timber on my toe, and when father paid him for his work the man gave me a gold dollar. I have never spent that dollar, but should have done so to buy a pocket-book, when nine years old, had not the family persuaded me to keep it.

I wish to emphasize the fact that any special privileges I have had came from good training, and not from any native genius, or lucky chances—I am what I was taught to **be**. With the same training some of my schoolmates had, I fear I should not have done as well as they did.

There were four of us children, and our school days began in a log schoolhouse. I well remember getting a whipping with another boy for picking the dried mud from the logs and throwing it at other pupils. We were smart boys, like many others, and like them were afraid people would not find it out unless we did some foolish thing. The teacher used the switch argument and won the case—it is about the only argument worth anything with a smart boy of that age. I knew too much to take any case of school discipline home with me; my father thought a boy could keep out of trouble if he behaved himself, and I was sent to school with the idea that the teacher was to be obeyed. My parents never asked us if we wanted to go to school, or to church; both were taken as a matter of course. It was not school or fishing, it was school or hard work, and plenty of argument against growing up a dunce. When my brother and I had completed the studies taught in the country school, we were sent to Baraboo to a select or private school—a good school, taught by Christian teachers. We hired a room and did part of our own cooking. This was a lesson in good sense and economy, and served me well later. My father died when I was sixteen years old, leaving my brother and myself to take charge of the farm. We took turns in going to school until it was decided that I should study all the year, and help was hired to take my place on the farm.

I graduated from the Baraboo High School, entered the State University in the autumn of 1872, and graduated from that institution in 1876. I wanted to become a teacher of modern languages, and accordingly went to Germany the following September. I remained abroad three years, dividing my time between Marburg and Leipzig, in Germany, and between Geneva and Paris while making French a specialty. I used the vacations in travel, one of which included an extended tour in Italy.

It was in Leipzig that I first met my wife, Sarah Thacher Cook, the daughter of a Congregational minister. At that time, in company with her aunt and cousin, she was studying music and German, and enjoying the opportunities of travel on the continent. Our acquaintance was continued the next winter in Geneva, where she had gone to study French, and I to pursue my studies in the university, and it was on the shores of Lake Geneva, with Mount Blanc and the Jura Mountains in view, that we became engaged. Returning home in 1879, I spent part of the next year studying Norse at the Wisconsin University, and was married in the summer of 1881. After teaching five years, I decided to enter the ministry of the Methodist Church, and consequently took the three-years' theological course at Evanston, Ill. Since then I have spent twenty years in the active ministry and three years in the travels already mentioned.

OUR FAMILY LIFE.

A brief account of our family life will aid in explaining more fully my idea of the practical application of the self-mastery system.

Two children came to our home: Edward, born August 12, 1882; and Margaret, born May 17, 1887. With a son and a daughter, our promise of home-life was very complete, but of short duration. Margaret remained with us only a few months, and then passed on to the next world to continue the life so brief here. My earnest prayer on that October night, when we knew the final parting must soon come, was that something of the sweetness and gentleness of the life then passing from earth might enter into mine and there live and flourish. I determined to do everything I could to make the way safe for all the daughters of earth, that they might have a chance to become what I had hoped my own daughter would be—a noble Christian woman. With this thought in mind, I began to investigate the social-purity movement, visited the medical schools in Chicago, and sought conferences with specialists to inform myself more thoroughly on this topic. I continued my labors in this field for some years, when my wife took up that subject as her special line of work, and I began the general studies of the home and its needs.

My son, Edward Penn Smith, graduated from the Madison High School in 1900, and from Lawrence College in 1905.

When a very small boy, he was taught to work and earn money, and also to save it for some good purpose. His mother and I both knew that habit is built up by teaching from some person, and so took good care never to teach him that a cent meant candy or gum. He never wasted money on either liquor or tobacco, but, on the other hand, he invested his savings where they could be earning something for a college course. He became a Christian in childhood, and joined the church when about eleven years old. As a boy he had worked on a farm during most of his summer vacations, and early began to say he wanted to become a farmer. After graduating from college, he took a three-years' course in agriculture at the Wisconsin University to better fit him for his chosen calling. Declining a more lucrative position in the North, he went South to labor among the colored people, and became superintendent of the large farm connected with Talladega College, in Alabama. Energetic, not afraid of any kind of work, and eager to practice and teach the best methods of farming, he had made an excellent beginning there, and his work and faithfulness were highly commended by the professors and managers of the institution.

In July, 1912, he was married to Lucy Emily Ayers, a cultured young woman, who was a teacher in the same college. In October of that year, on our way to Cuba, we visited them in their happy home. Everything was full of promise for the future, and a large element in my travels and studies was to establish in the mind of my son the firm conviction that Christian service to the world is the only worthy aim in life. Indeed, I was even then preparing to write a book with this purpose largely in view. We went on our way after a few weeks' pleasant sojourn in their home, spent some time in Cuba, and then continued our journey to Mexico.

The latter part of December we were staying in Orizaba, Mexico, when one morning that messenger so much welcomed and dreaded by turns, brought a brief note from the telegraph announcing the almost incredible tidings that our son, our only remaining child, was dead. Only those who have gone through the same experience know what that meant to us. In one sense it came at a merciful time. We were away in a strange land, greatly absorbed in mission work, and there were no associations about us to remind us of our loss. There was nothing to be done but to go on with our work and bear what could not be avoided. I thought of the many thousands of young men whom I had seen in the prisons of the world, and I knew their parents were more to be pitied than we were. All these things were of assistance to us, but the terrible fact remained. It takes time to adjust one's self to a great loss. I always like to observe children, and now began to notice that they would often look at me with serious faces, and then sometimes run away. I was surprised at this and tried to find out why they seemed afraid. I took the mirror and studied my own face. I could see no joy there; it was not a face to attract a child. Then I said to myself, "This will not do; if I have lost my own children, I must not wear so sad a face as to repel other children." So I began to make myself more cheerful and to live in the joy of the young life about me.

REASON FOR THIS SKETCH.

Now I come to the chief reason for writing this sketch. It touches the principles of self-mastery and the Christian life in a very vital way. Here is the question, "Did God have anything special to do with the loss of our children; did He take them out of the world by any direct act?" My answer is that He did not. I do not know the cause of the death of my daughter. My son was drowned by accidentally slipping where no danger could have been expected. God was not instrumental in his falling to his death—it was a case of the ten-thousandth time which was fatal, while all before had been passed safely. My belief is that at the present time God takes practically no one out of this world by direct act. If He did, the list would be different. The forms of our expression, as well as the quite general belief of men, make God the doer of all that ends life here. I believe this is a very serious error, and for this reason: If God does it, He knows best, and we must submit; if man does it, we ought, in a large number of cases, to learn better, and then live by that higher knowledge. God will deal justly with each of us who pass out of this life; but if we go before our time, we may be found standing at the door of eternity very poorly fitted to enter that realm.

As a Christian minister I have come in touch with many a person who was carrying a great grievance against God for taking some loved one, and who had become gloomy and would not try to cheer up. For one to grieve thus is wrong, it is unreasonable, it is putting the blame in the wrong place; and instead of becoming wiser for some future event, the mourner only wears deeper the rut of error in which he is moving. The world is beginning to ask seriously, What is the cause of this and that early death? We have here a very important question, and one worthy of careful study. In some misjudged cases the parents, in their youth or later, may have broken some of God's laws of health, and the early death of the child was the result of their lack of knowledge.

I hope I am understood. I do not at all blame God for the desolation of my home in the loss of both of my children, for He is my great comfort. I know He has my treasures, and He will keep them safely until I follow on to meet and greet them. I care very much what my children think of my course in this life, and my task now is to make it easy for them to say, when we stand face to face, "Father, we rejoice in your record as it has been brought to us by the coming of those whom you have helped; we are glad that you did not charge God wrongfully, nor sit down and mourn because of losing us, but gave the earthly affection, the care, the labors we no longer needed, to the great world of children who did need them."

We do not consider ourselves childless, for we have adopted the childhood of the whole world as ours. I take into my arms some child from as many nations as possible; it may be a Chinese, an Indian, a Japanese, a Mexican, or any one within reach. One day, away in the mountains of North Africa, I took the hand of a little Kabyle boy of two years—a Mohammedan child. The boy smiled, and the father seemed pleased, though neither of us knew a syllable of the other's spoken language. I think the smile must be a part of God's language, for all can understand it.

I have in conclusion a most earnest word of appeal to the many persons who have lost one or more children, to those who have had none, and especially to those who, like us, have lost all. You who have time, talent, or money, devote as much as you can to some line of human betterment in the great world of the young. I give you my testimony that it makes a plain couch like a bed of down, and changes a simple fare into a banquet, to feel that the money thus saved is turned to the good of those young enough to be easily helped. I call this not charity, nor a gift, but a wise investment; and such an investment places me among the rich men of the earth.

As a parting word, and in the name of our beloved children, I plead with you to forget the unattractive exterior of many of the parents, and remember the children who need our love. Come with me into this field of the world, and we will gather our arms full of these flowers to lay at the feet of the Master who loves them, and who will teach us the larger lesson of love for all humanity.

CPSIA information can be obtained
at www.ICGtesting.com
Printed in the USA
BVHW040842040219
539406BV00023B/276/P

9 781331 857228